Assessment in Arts Education

Edited by Philip Taylor

D1571238

HEINEMANN
Portsmouth, NH

Heinemann
A division of Reed Elsevier Inc.
361 Hanover Street
Portsmouth, NH 03801–3912
www.heinemann.com

Offices and agents throughout the world

Library of Congress Cataloging-in-Publication Data
Assessment in arts education / edited by Philip Taylor; with a foreword by Joe Kincheloe.
       p. cm.
  Includes bibliographical references.
  ISBN-10: 0-325-00795-0
  ISBN-13: 978-0-325-00795-3
  1. Arts—Study and teaching. 2. Educational evaluation. I. Taylor, Philip.
  NX282.A87 2006
  700.71—dc22   2006019539

Editor: Lisa A. Barnett
Production service: Lisa S. Garboski, bookworks
Production coordinator: Sonja S. Chapman
Cover design: Jenny Jensen Greenleaf
Compositor: TechBooks
Manufacturing: Louise Richardson

Printed in the United States of America on acid-free paper
10   09   08   07   06   VP   1   2   3   4   5

To Dorothy Heathcote and Maxine Greene, two women who have made a difference in the artistic lives of young and older people.

Contents

Foreword

On first glance, the title of Philip Taylor's new book poses on oxy-moronic question: how does one assess arts education? That question asked, Philip and his colleagues answer in the critical, socially just way that one would hope. Not an easy task, these authors discuss the ambiguities and complexities involved in *assessing* arts. Traumatized by the taint of the No Child Left Behind scars, educators are seeking to equalize their own dignity, the arts curriculum, the rampant deskilling of teachers, and the antiaesthetic nature of NCLB. As Philip mentions in his introduction, now is the time, more than ever, that we must heed the call of the arts.

How do we accommodate an objectives-based learning? Evidence-based learning? Data-driven standardized testing? And the arts?

Numbers-crunching test advocates are convinced that rigor cannot exist without measurement driven by both politicians and fear-filled school administrators. There is an innate refusal to acknowledge that any learning can take place without strict measurement. The authors in this book advocate rigorous education, disciplined education, an education with the consciousness that learning and the *craft* of the arts can be done with intelligent assessment. Evidence-based assessment is an affront to rigor. It spits in the face of rigor, using the word promiscuously as political doublespeak, while the arts advocates and teachers who speak for the children and youth they teach live in fear of being "caught" teaching something meaningful.

Acknowledging that each teaching venue is unique and specific, the authors in this collection discuss the ways that the arts can be taught and facilitated without losing the essential nature of the aesthetic. Using a premise based in critical pedagogy, arts teachers can name the overt curriculum of NCLB and teach an authentic curriculum at the same time. A challenging task, critical teachers must be aware of the centers of power within school administration, the goals of assessment, yet teach their students without the cloud of positivist measurement hanging needlessly over each project. Rigorous teaching does not discount assessment, it creates contextual assessment.

Philip Taylor is an educator who takes seriously the arts, justice, and rigorous pedagogy. One only has to look at the quality of his students to understand the power of his teaching and his scholarship. This volume is a tribute to the work in educational theatre and the arts to which Philip is dedicated. It is an honor to write this foreword.

Joe L. Kincheloe
Canada Research Chair
McGill University

Prologue and Acknowledgment

At a young age, around four or five, I had decided to be a teacher. That was that, and nothing would change my mind.

Teaching became centered in me because my family lived opposite an elementary school, and one of my best friends, Susan, was the janitor's daughter. Susan and I would follow her parents around the school as they attended to their cleaning and other chores. While they dusted and swept, we explored the empty classrooms, drew with chalk, and let our fanciful thoughts run wild. I would imagine I was the teacher, and Susan was my class. I gave her lots of assignments, which I loved, although I did notice that when the roles were reversed, and she was my teacher, I did not take too kindly to her instruction.

One of the first Christmas presents I remember receiving as a child was a chalkboard; we called them blackboards back then. Such a gift was formative for me as my role-playing as teacher grew to new heights. When I wasn't organizing puppet shows for the neighborhood children, or playing in my cubby house, I was in my bedroom enacting school. My imaginary class was not always well behaved, however, and I recall taking the recalcitrants into the bathroom and smacking them with a leather belt, which had a frightening crackerjack sound. I think I learned how to do that from my father who was known for being quite the disciplinarian.

So, it was no surprise to anyone that I became quite proficient in theatre at my public high school. I took drama class every year, and always auditioned for, and often managed to get, the lead roles, including my favorite, Jimmy Porter, in John Osborne's *Look Back in Anger*. While I loved the thrill of performing, the call to teach was greater. I was fortunate that one of the top teacher education programs was only a short bus ride from my house, and it was at this college where my real excitement for teaching began.

Unlike bell hooks (1994) who was greatly turned off by her college years, I was exposed to teachers who were highly committed, and challenged me, for the most part, to become an engaged professional. Perhaps this interest had something to do with the progressive education movement Australia inherited from England in the 1970s, but equally I do not recall suffering the sense of alienation or the pangs of the outcast that hooks did. Being a white male I was a member of the privileged elite. Yet, isn't it odd that while being gay, I don't recall feeling concerned that the issues of queer kids were never addressed at college. Perhaps it was because I wasn't out then, a gutless stance I regret today, but to my family I figured I would've been a big disappointment, or I worried about the response to a *poofta* (Australian slang for homosexual) being in the house, and maybe I wanted to be straight anyway. So I, like many others, lived the pretense, and kept hidden a seismic part of my being.

I do remember wondering at teachers' college how the one person of color in my drama education courses, a black woman from South Africa, felt about the difference by which she was surrounded. Australia was and largely still is, very white and heteronormative in its outlook, and struggles with what multiculturalism actually entails, even though the public rhetoric would have you believe otherwise. For the most part, I put those wonders aside, strange admission I know, and focused on school drama. It was here that I encountered the brilliant theatre praxis of Dorothy Heathcote, who was the first to teach me the power of tolerating ambiguity in the classroom, and the ways in which I could structure for evolving, shifting, and often contradictory viewpoints. I went onto high school teaching, directed shows and after-school theatre clubs. But, I was never entirely happy, felt alienated by formal schooling, didn't relate to the macho homophobic culture, and decided I needed to leave the land down under for a time, and head off to New York! Where else?

It was really in this great city that my new education began. I discovered the potent meaning of diversity and disenfranchisement; it was there right in front of me. I saw my white skin for the first time, and recognized my privileges, my power, and my access. I discovered the work of Paulo Freire and Maxine Greene, and began to understand the key tenets that shape a critical aesthetic education:

questioning the routine, accommodating multiple frames, being dialogical, and grounding the arts in contextual experience. My eyes had been opened to the other, the silent, and the marginalized, and through theatre education, issues pertaining to social justice and equity, the forgotten and voiceless, could be most eloquently explored. I am forever grateful to all those teachers who enabled me to see what previously I could not.

And, so, many years later, after a long period of teaching in Australian higher education, and returning to New York, I find myself in American teacher-education, struggling still to tolerate ambiguity. I work with extraordinarily gifted and determined students who are passionate to make a difference in the lives of young people, and in the communities in which they work—schools, shelters, seniors' centers, prisons.

However, something is different this time around. I find that most of my energies are occupied by administrative errands, faculty assignments, budget reports, five-year plans. I am constantly trying to justify my life's work, and that of my colleagues and students. I am burdened by the ever-increasing statistical printouts: charts on enrollment data, upward and downward changes (I mostly hear about the downward), Scholastic Aptitude and Graduate Record Examination scores, student application trends, the grinding paperwork associated with various audits. I see trepidation in the eyes of my collaborators as they try, so hard, to fall into line, to impress, and not rock the boat; fitting and squeezing their teaching into bite size, Chicken McNugget, pieces.

These are a few indicators and consequences of the movement called evidence-based learning: juggling the numbers, presenting the business plans, managing the annual reviews and inspections; oh dear, the dreaded accountability, and the prevailing fear it generates.

How, I wonder, will the arts deal with this new era? How will we ever be able to standardize the toleration of ambiguity?

I want to express my appreciation to the contributors to this book who will help us muster the arguments to deal with the current national obsession for evidence-based learning. It was not easy bringing all these artforms together, so I am grateful to the contributors for their patience and perseverance. There were numerous times when I thought I can't be bothered proceeding with this text, assessment is so dry, and who is really interested anyway? But, in those moments, I would come across yet another article on No

Child Left Behind, and be dismayed by the next round of published school test results. Now, more than ever, the call to bring back an artistic-aesthetic curriculum that privileges the voices of all our students, and their teachers, and not just the privileged and white, the straight and staid, is much needed. *Assessment in Arts Education* will help in that effort.

I am grateful to Joe Kincheloe for his powering scholarship, and for his fervent championing of the equitable. His reminder to us in teacher education to reskill our student teachers, permitting them to generate their own aesthetic sensibility is timely. Too often we deskill our students, relegating them to functionary servants whose only role is to moderate external standards, and to deliver uninspiring, predetermined, market-driven, and illogical lesson plans!

My great thanks to the late Lisa Barnett, who supported three projects of mine in the arts, and who was especially patient with this one. Fortunately, we had an editor in our field, and have a publishing house, who commissions educational textbooks in the arts that do not have to focus on how we deliver Level Three outcomes!

But, most of all, I would like to acknowledge Susan, my five-year-old Australian playmate from the neighboring school, who joined in on my dramatic play, many years ago, and gave me permission to imagine, and to dream . . . and to share, in time, my excitement and surprise with so many others.

Philip Taylor
New York City

WORK CITED

Hooks, b. 1994. *Teaching to Transgress: Education as the Practice of Freedom.* New York: Routledge.

Introduction: Assessment in Arts Education

Philip Taylor

We are in the midst of a rather unnerving time in arts education. On the one hand, it appears that the important lobbying of the National Arts Education Associations has enabled the arts disciplines to have a significant profile at the federal level. The membership of local, state, and national networks in art, dance, music, and visual art have argued tirelessly and convincingly to ensure their constituencies' interests are well represented. When I attended the annual meeting of the American Alliance for Theatre and Education recently, it was clear from the various breakout presentations and discussions that the commitment and passion to raising the profile of the arts across the country was strong. The contributors to this volume equally reveal the robust activity in promoting the other arts disciplines of dance, music, and visual art. They analyze the breadth of scholarship and research in their respective fields, the attention that is being paid to crafting curriculum policy frameworks, and the efforts made to ensure that school communities and society at large benefit from an arts entitlement.

As well, departments of education and school boards are establishing position papers to assist the implementation of K–12 arts experiences. In New York City, for instance, the department of education has appointed directors in the four arts disciplines, as well as supporting the creation of so-called "Blueprints," which aim to support and inform teachers' and students' learning (www.nycenet.edu/projects). Now arts teachers, like their math and language arts colleagues, can hold up a city-sanctioned document and present it in faculty meetings. Teacher certification in all arts disciplines has seen a gradual rise in the number of teaching positions becoming available in the New York City public school system. At NYU, for example, in my discipline of educational theatre, our enrollments have risen from

160 to 250 students in the period of eight years, and most of these students want to gain a license to teach theatre in public schools. It is indeed helpful to them, and our faculty of course, when they can advocate for their discipline with principals and administrators, school boards and parents, on the basis that the state and city educational authorities proclaim arts experiences in our schools have to be offered.

Furthermore, numerous government and private agencies, including the National Endowment for the Arts, the U.S. Department of Education, the Dana Foundation, and the J. Paul Getty Trust, are providing grants and sponsoring programs that support the arts in schools (Rabkin, 2004). The American Educational Research Association now has a special interest group committed to arts-based research. And perhaps most gratifying of all, for some, was when the arts were declared for the first time a "core" academic subject under the No Child Left Behind (NCLB) Act of 2001, which Congress signed into law on January 8, 2002 . Some heaved a huge sigh of relief, and many celebrated (MacPherson, 2004). It seemed that all the good efforts had borne fruit, and, at last, the arts had found a permanent platform in both the political and educational arenas. Ah, yes, life was good if you were a U.S. arts educator; or, was it?

While it is clear that we have played well the game of good citizenship and that our efforts at representation have brought tremendous dividends, there has been a considerable compromise. That compromise and how we can best manage it is the focus of this book, *Assessment in Arts Education*.

COMPROMISES AND BENCHMARKS

The ultimate compromise can be best characterized by a prioritized concern with the rubric, the standard, the apparent need to neutralize teachers' professional judgments, and to silence children out of their own learning. I observe this situation frequently in schools with the focus on endpoints, benchmarks, and attainment targets. As teachers begin their lessons by writing statements on the chalkboard of what students will be able to do, and then proceed to work through activities in linear progression, I see fairly mechanical work with no animation. Students are constantly being reminded of what is expected from them and the implications of the NCLB legislation are forever in sight. The only "true" measure of achievement under this federal law is that gained by "scientifically rigorous evidence," which merges from a neopositivist paradigm (see Taylor 1996 for how this paradigm impacts upon teachers' understanding of arts education).

Scientifically rigorous connotes a concentration on the clinical, on statistical measurement, and comparison of control and treatment groups. In NCLB, the "effectiveness" of any teaching intervention can only be determined by "the randomized controlled trial." In a rather alarming document for arts educators, "Identifying and Implementing Educational Practices Supported by Rigorous Evidence: A User-Friendly Guide" (Coalition for Evidence-Based Policy, 2003) examples are provided. Readers should note that I have substituted art for math, in the following definition:

[handwritten margin note: USER-FRIENDLY RIGOR?]

> Randomized controlled trials are studies that randomly assign individuals to an intervention group or to a control group, in order to measure the effects of the intervention. For example, suppose you want to test, in a randomized controlled trial, whether a new (art) curriculum for third-graders is more effective than your school's existing (art) curriculum for third-graders. You would randomly assign a large number of third-grade students to either an intervention group, which uses the new curriculum, or to a control group, which uses the existing curriculum. You would then measure the (art) achievement of both groups over time. The difference in (art) achievement between the two groups would represent the effect of the new curriculum compared to the existing curriculum. (1)

[handwritten margin notes: 2003 / ALL QUANT, / No QUAL / THE TEACHER, NOT THE CURRICULUM. / IT'S THE TEACHER, STUPID.]

Comparative analysis seems to be the way of the future, with random selection of children participating in experimental trials. In the above definition, words like *control, random, measure, large number*, and *effect* grow out of an empiricist's logic where the need to quantify and neutralize human identity is foremost. Presumably, high achievement refers to an increase in numerical test scores. Note, there are no references to small-scale case studies, context-based learning, and descriptive reporting. Teacher research, action inquiry, and reflective practice clearly have no place in this scientific paradigm.

It is perplexing indeed for arts educators to think in terms of such controls and treatments, especially given that arts experiences are constructed by contextual circumstances and the social health of any given classroom. How do we reduce an arts curriculum, powered by metaphysical realities, and subjective aesthetic encounters, to a series of discrete propositional outcomes? How do we test whether a grade three art curriculum is more effective in one school as compared to another? Sadly, the subjective and interpretive have no role to play in a scientifically rigorous era that emphasizes objective products that can be tabulated and then generalized from one school population to the next.

At the very least, it appears dehumanizing to set up rigidly controlled experiments to explore the success of new teaching "interventions" that include one cohort of students, known as the control group, in a new program, while another cohort is denied access to it. Ironically, all the initial enthusiasm for the arts being represented in NCLB has turned to frustration, given that reading and math are to be the two subjects tested annually. Such has seen a gradual diminution in the offerings of arts programs in some school districts because of the need to prepare students for those annual tests. The National Art Education Association, for instance, has prepared a booklet, "Tips for Parent Advocacy," which MacPherson claims will assist parents to "lobby for arts education in their schools," while the Arts Education Partnership has produced a guide, "No Subject Left Behind," which articulates how the arts can play a role in academic success, presumably in the service of the mainstream curriculum (MacPherson, 2004).

In my view, it is to our advantage that the arts aren't subjected to the NCLB examinations. The impact of such infatuation with national testing and benchmarks has had major fallout, and reduced dance, music, theatre, and visual arts teachers to package their curriculum as a series of bulleted points and levels of achievement. Numerous examples are contained in this book. We have even heard recently of a federal higher education commission exploring the introduction of standardized testing in universities and colleges "to prove that students are learning and to allow easier comparisons on quality" (Arenson, 2006, 1). *Proof* of learning, it appears, is connected to the "rigorous" generation of comparative neutralized test results which must appear unambiguous and crystal clear. A business executive chairs The Commission on the Future of Higher Education, and the head of the test-coaching company Kaplan Inc. is one of its members. One might have thought there was a potential conflict of interest having the director of a testing agency adjudicating whether nationwide testing should be introduced into colleges.

UGH

"The unanswered question in higher education is," stated one commissioner, "How good is the product?" He went on to say: "A growing number of people want answers. What higher education is about to learn is that they can't play the 'trust me' game anymore" (20). Rhetoric like this shows that crucial decisions about educational processes are no longer being made by the ones on the front line, the colleges, the schools, the teachers, and their students. The weighty decisions are being thrashed out in business. Within this context, the marketplace will determine what should be taught in schools and how. And evidently business distrusts the voices and instincts of the educators.

Jonathan Kozol in his landmark text, *The Shame of the Nation: The Restoration of Apartheid Schooling in America*, researched how such testing discriminates against black and Hispanic children, and other groups who are disadvantaged by norm and criterion-based referencing. The testing regime reinforces the interests of privileged white and heteronormative culture with its emphasis on functional literacy, canonized texts, and traditional mainstreaming approaches to instruction. There are no opportunities for individualized learning or catering to particular classroom communities. Students who aren't skilled at taking the tests, their teachers, and the schools they attend will be labeled as performing below the basic standard. Consequently, school budgets will be cut, with a view to closing schools down if they do not improve on their test score. When NCLB refers to empowering parents to make decisions about their children's education, increasing parental choice and opportunity, the message seems clear: Review your schools' overall score and ranking, and if not satisfied, move your child out, if you can! But NCLB provides little advice on how so-called "low achieving" schools will ever be able to succeed at improving their ranking.

Hours of class time are devoted to preparing students to take the tests, which often have no bearing on the curriculum imperatives teachers and students want to pursue. "I want to change the face of reading instruction across the United States from an art to a science," says an assistant to the former education secretary (quoted in Kozol, 78). "There's something crystal clear about a number," says another. If we subscribe to Maxine Greene's (1978) vision that the arts are for reenvisioning new possibilities, for disclosing the previously unimaginable, for enabling our students to have a voice, and to demonstrate their relationship to the world, it is hard for us to have confidence in scientific models of training that reduce the role of teachers to delivering a checklist.

"There must be attending," writes Greene, highlighting the role of the arts curriculum to heighten students' perceptual abilities to reflect both in and on artworks:

> . . . there must be noticing, at once, there must be a reflective turn-ing back to the streams of consciousness—the stream that contains our perceptions, our reflections, yes, and our ideas. Clearly this end-in-view cannot be predetermined. I am arguing for self-reflective-ness, however, and new disclosures, as I am arguing for critical reflection at a moment of stasis and crystallized habit. If the unique-ness of the artistic-aesthetic can be reaffirmed, if we can consider futuring as we combat immersion, old either/ors may disappear. We may make possible a pluralism of visions, a multiplicity of realities. We may enable those we teach to rebel. (182)

In the NCLB world order, there can be no "uniqueness" of the arts curriculum. School programs have to conform to the external dictates of the objectified curriculum. In this respect, assessment moves away from its traditional role of ongoing monitoring of teachers' and students' relationship to the work, a kind of infor-mal review of whether the group is managing the tasks at hand, and what assistance they might require in order to more ably com-plete them. Assessment becomes evaluation, and the two words are used interchangeably. Formative assessments disappear in the new regime, and the role of the teacher is to be the judge and make final exit statements on ability. There is little time for reflec-tive praxis and no need for peer and self-assessments. The mar-ketplace doesn't allow it. Any idea that the arts present alternate realities, that they "rebel" against the familiar and the mundane, have to be stifled. In this respect, the arts, if they are to survive, have to be functional agents that serve the goals of industry and business.

Kozol argues that the dominant longing of turning art into sci-ence pervades every aspect of schooling. He tells the story of how even the usual practices of children filing to lunch or recess are "subjected to the same determined emphasis upon empirical preci-sion." In one school, for example, he observed how teachers were expected to grade students on how orderly they were as they

moved from one room to another. There were thirty-two filing categories;   *Boy, THIS MAKES ME*
                                                      SICK

> "Line leader confidently leads the class. . . Line is straight. . . Spacing
> is tight. . . The class is stepping together. . . Everyone shows pride,
> their shoulders high. . ., no slumping," according to the strict criteria
> for filing at Level 4.
> "Line is straight, but one or two people (are) not quite in line,"
> according to the box for Level 3. "Line leader leads the class," but
> not "with confidence" this time, and "almost everyone shows
> pride. . ." (79)

And so forth, right down to Level One: "Line leader is paying no
attention. . . Heads are turning every way. . . Hands are touching. . .
The line is not straight. . . There is no pride." This was no joke,
writes Kozol. These instructions had been printed in a handbook
for the teachers of a large urban city school.

Inevitably a dehumanizing process is at work here, as students
and teachers are expected to tow the straight and narrow. There
are few opportunities for thinking and acting outside of the regime,
and schools become military-like in their determination to pursue
the linear and categorical. It saddens me to go to schools and hear
of the fear and frustration governing teachers' lives. With contracts
at risk of being canceled, and promotion and tenure decisions
placed in the hands of the external committees who feel duty bound
to enforce such scientifically rigorous mandates, one wonders how
an arts curriculum can ever privilege aesthetic processes committed
to sustained and probing exploration of the human condition.

I become disenchanted when I speak to teachers who feel obliged
to create notice boards and banners listing a series of bulleted
points on what students should be able to do, how well, and
whether they are achieving at a basic, proficient, or advanced level.
This obsession with outcomes paralyzes arts educators from activating their classrooms as sites for critical thinking. Kincheloe (2005)
agrees and describes this process as a gradual deskilling of teachers:

> . . . teachers and other professionals often fall into a state of
> degraded professional practice when hyperrationalized reforms
> remove the conceptualization of the professsional task from its exe-
> cution. Deskilling positions teachers as low-level functionaries in the

educational workplace who simply follow the dictates of their administrative superiors. (114)

How then do we address this imbalance? If the gains of the arts community have led to inevitable compromises on what an artistic-aesthetic curriculum should be like, how then do we get back to first principles, and help reskill teachers, students, parents, and the wider community, into understanding what is really worth knowing and being able to do in the arts?

FIRST PRINCIPLES: HOW SHOULD EVIDENCE-BASED LEARNING IN THE ARTS LOOK?

The contributors to this book describe how the marketplace economy and the political agenda to enforce businesslike accountability in schools have resulted in educators losing confidence in their own artistic intelligence. We have known for some time how crucial the teacher is to providing a rich scaffolding for students to discover what powers an aesthetic sensibility (Elliott, 1991/1998). Just because a grade six dance student can demonstrate some of Laban's techniques or a senior appears to have a sophisticated dramaturgical grasp of the theatre of the absurd movement is not sufficient or compelling evidence that they are evolving their own critical faculties in the arts. Such representations merely reveal that they have apparently mastered a particular task.

Evidence-based learning should move beyond identifying the discrete skills that students reveal at any particular time, and concentrate on how they are embedding them within their own evolving aesthetic sensibility. The authors in this collection are advocating for a commitment to interrelatedness, a desire to search for connection and disconnections; in other words, a kind of lateral curriculum that enables students to scrutinize, to interrogate, to release their own imaginations, and, therein, get closer to their own artistic vision.

Certainly, our students will be baffled, at times, and be thrown into states of disequilibria, and they will be frustrated by nonlinear and abstract artforms, where meanings are not immediately apparent, and where they see no artistic merit in a particular artifact. And, yes, they will question and debate, and fail to reach consensus, and there will always be those on the outside who find nothing of interest in current practice, being more content to experiment with their own materials and how these can shape an inner landscape. But surely such is the hallmark of an artistic-aesthetic curriculum. The arts have historically been nonconforming and operate outside of a mainstreaming functional agenda, as Kozol reminds us:

> Many of the brightest, most creative, independent-minded, and ambitious kids I know are not "team-players" and don't *want* to be and, indeed, would lose the very essence of what makes them full, complex, and interesting people if they were. There will, I am afraid, be fewer fascinating mavericks, fewer penetrating question-ers, and fewer powerful dissenters coming from our inner-city schools before too long if this agenda cannot be reversed. Team players may well be of great importance to the operation of a busi-ness corporation and they are obviously essential in the military services; but a healthy nation needs its future poets, prophets, ribald scientists, and maddening iconoclasts at least as much as it needs people who will file in a perfect line to an objective they are told they cannot question. (106)

Assessment in Arts Education examines the principles that should be guiding the documentation of human achievement in an evidence-based era. It is a book that contests mythologies surrounding what is effective, valid, and reliable evidence. The spurious claims that are made about measurement, particularly the notion that quantifi-cation is the only scientifically rigorous method, are explored. From the chapters that follow, I have identified themes of concern to the authors:

First principles in evidence-based learning need to put teachers and students in touch with their own aesthetic consciousness where subjective and intrapersonal processes of art-making are at the forefront. Clearly, an arts curriculum has to be informed by those great choreographers, musicians, painters, and playwrights, and their various artistic col-laborators, who have shaped and informed our cultural heritage, past and present, and as we move into the future. Our contributors are not arguing that notions of criteria and excellence are redun-dant or unnecessary in an arts curriculum, but rather we need to be adeptly creative in assisting students to evolve their principles in taste, judgment, and value.

First principles in evidence-based learning recognize that artists have important things to say about the world, and that the knowledge systems that those meanings are communicated through are mostly in symbolic and metaphorical forms. I was reminded here of the formative work of Elliott Eisner who was helped generations of arts educators get in touch with their inner streams of consciousness. "The selection of a form through which the world is to be represented," claims Eisner (quoted in Finley, 2005), "not only influences what humans can say but also influences what they are likely to experience" (685). First principles should help our students understand the relationship of form to content, and how artworks operate as mediated depictions able to transport us to unique imaginary realms.

First principles in evidence-based learning acknowledge that the teacher provides important scaffolding on artistic-aesthetic sensibility. Teachers will feel confident sharing their own aesthetic praxis, they will understand the transformative role that artworks have made throughout time, and will structure encounters in their classrooms that empower students to experience their full potential as artists, and as commentators on their own and others' work. First principles accept that teachers are professionals capable of generating their own criteria while simultaneously moderating the criteria of others, when and where appropriate.

First principles in evidence-based learning accept that there are common and different ways in which students can demonstrate their relationship to the work and to their evolving aesthetic sensibility. Educators need to explore ways of capturing the internal life of their students, and how this influences the quality of participation in the arts classroom. First principles commit to the idea that arts classrooms are sites for action, reflection, and transformation. In this respect, teachers and students are operating as reflective practitioners who join together in an artistic community. First principles acknowledge that each classroom is fundamentally different and unique. The social context of the classroom often shapes what is possible, and evidence-based learners need to consider that arts attainment does not occur in a vacuum.

Four outstanding U.S. leaders from the arts disciplines, Edward Warburton (dance), David Elliott (music), Robert Landy (theatre), and Stephanie Springgay (visual art), now tackle head-on how assessment has been construed within their own artform. They describe the historical and dominant currents in assessment practices, the controversies, and how the current administrative climate is impacting upon teachers' work. They make suggestions of how teachers might think of assessment in an outcomes-based era.

Drawing on the lead chapters in each arts discipline, Christina Hong (dance), Richard Colwell (music), Renée Kredell (visual art), and I (theatre) each present our observations of assessment practices in our discipline. An important component of these responses is that they bring further experiences into the discussion. In some instances, there is agreement about the state of play and how educators might adapt their pedagogy so that they can play the accountability game and survive. In other cases, there is a disagreement about such matters as the importance of the standards, the purposes of an arts curriculum, the function of the teacher, and what knowledge students should be able to demonstrate. I believe readers will find these chapters useful and possibly provocative as they begin to formulate or consolidate their own positions on the kind of compelling evidence that is required in arts education assessment.

Dance Education

Edward Warburton launches our discussion by investigating how dance education had been predominantly viewed as an essentialist "talent" imperative. You either had the skill to dance or not, and the cattle call audition would determine if you could cut it with the best of them. Recent studies in human and cognitive development, Warburton claims, have debunked this essentialist myth, and explored other constructivist viewpoints. He canvasses the qualities of authentic assessment and how "intelligence-fair" assessments should be ongoing, and then differentiates between educational, professional and "dance as art" curricular models. Warburton examines the evolution of the standards movement and how it impacts dance in schools. He highlights the value of self-assessments and posits that standardization works against "individual and local community values in aesthetic production and response."

Christina Hong argues in response to Warburton that assessment is central to the teaching and learning enterprise in dance education. She draws a distinction between "assessment of learning," viewing this primarily as summative, used for purposes of grading and reporting, and "assessment for learning," which she sees as benefiting the students in their lifelong projects. Hong describes convergent and divergent assessment, and claims that curriculum outputs provide a buffer for teachers and students. She references the New Zealand arts curriculum, which she helped construct. One key aspect of the New Zealand curriculum is its notion of dance literacy, defined as "thinking and communicating in, through, and about the dance art form." Hong claims that the development of national exemplars assists teachers in making qualitative assessments of their own students.

Music Education

David Elliott poses some of the challenges music educators face in a standards-based era. As schools become major conglomerations for business and pay heed to the marketplace, teachers are losing sight of what music-making actually entails. Highlighting some of the flaws in the drive for objective measurements, a movement Elliott argues is powered by white, conservative, and right-wing sentiments, interest in a critical and creative pedagogy has flown out the window. Music teachers spend far too long teaching to the test, and trying to implement programs in which they have had little investment writing. Elliott documents the weaknesses in *The School Music Program,* which has sugarcoated the complexity in developing an imaginative and empowering music education. The dominant perspective, he writes, is shaped by a "crisis-style 'advocacy mindset' that packages and repackages music to fit the latest ideology." Elliott proposes a "praxial philosophy" that highlights "musical values and musical knowledge." Such a philosophy needs to be grounded in an education for life approach where there is clear connection between what occurs both in and out of school. Developing musical understanding (musicianship and listenership) is central to Elliott's thesis, and educators, he claims, need to be adept at facilitating such development while playing the game of satisfying the whims of the bureaucrats.

Richard Colwell argues, in response to Elliott, that standards are important for any field, including music, and that music educators need to accept this reality. He describes the history of public accountability, and how the knowledge base from which music educators have historically worked from is "shallow." Colwell provides an overview of how music programs have been assessed. He asks whether teachers can make trustworthy judgments about their students' ability, and suggests that teachers would benefit from an external judge or observer. Colwell is critical of the music content standards and the resources required in achieving them. He discusses the role of the teacher who should be "correcting, modeling, and providing feedback." This leads into a discussion of what teacher education programs should be aiming to achieve. "We need to be able to define incompetence in teaching," he writes, "and to develop a few diagnostic tools."

Theatre Education

Robert Landy identifies subjective assumptions that underpin creative arts processes. He posits that assessment and evaluation are more objective and tend to be based upon "specified criteria" associated with various theoretical models. Assessment has two purposes: to determine student readiness for certain dramatic tasks, and to gauge students' competency in drama. Evaluation is used during or after a process to determine the breadth and depth of learning. He argues that "age-based standards" can be adopted to "measure" whether students are performing on task. He provides an overview of the evolution of the drama education movement in the Western world, with its focus on subjective phenomenological processes, toward efforts to quantify learning experiences through behavioral objectives. He then draws parallels with the drama therapy movement and its psychological models. Landy provides numerous examples of assessments in drama therapy and how these might be incorporated in educational settings.

For my part, I argue that most assessments and evaluations fail to take into account the aesthetic dimension. Too many theatre educators are concerned with discrete skill deposits, principally because of the outcomes' orientation of most schools. Questions that ask, What is drama? What is art? need to be revisited. I assume a critical theorist posturing and demonstrate how teacher education should promote dialectical encounters. Linear approaches to lesson planning are deconstructed and the implications these have for arts education assessment are discussed. I assert that the standards era, with its concern for delivering a prepackaged content and skill kit, has actually deskilled teachers and students.

Visual Arts Education

Stephanie Springgay opens her chapter with a critique of the standards and how they impose a "mind and body" split. She discusses the fragmentation in curriculum and pedagogy within an outcomes-driven era, and identifies how teachers are disempowered when they have no control over negotiating what the benchmarks should be in their classrooms. For instance, the frequency of multiple choice tests delimits students' capacity to engage with their visual world. She points to some of the problems with teacher education programs that "instruct" students to begin their lessons with a list of outcomes, which negates the development of an aesthetic sensibility.

Springgay examines the body's role in the production of knowledge, a role marginalized in the current frameworks, and how universalist assumptions in curriculum policy fail to accommodate student diversity. She uses the metaphor of the fold, which is "interconnected, embracing touch and intercorporeality," to characterize what assessment should look like in the visual arts classroom. Springgay explores the role of tactile epistemologies in the visual arts classroom. She claims that relational knowing is necessary for personal and social reconstruction and transformation, and that most current assessment practices do not facilitate good questioning on creating, interrogating, and thinking through "art as bodied visual encounters."

Renée Kredell works from Victor Turner's notion of the liminal space to argue that human beings are always in a state of evolution, and these stages of growth, flux, and disruptions need to be privileged in assessment. Nonetheless, she believes that Springgay's plea for an embodied assessment appears "fanciful and unrealistic" given the NCLB act. Teachers need to look to the realities of mandated school reform while at the same time striving to achieve multilayered and qualitative assessments. While Kredell does not provide strategies as to how teachers might devise embodied assessments under NCLB, she is confident that educators can find a way of balancing standardized assessments with the nonstandardized.

WORKS CITED

Arenson, K. W. 2006. "Panel explores standards for Colleges." *The New York Times*, February 9: 1, 20.

Coalition for Evidence-Based Policy. 2003. "Identifying and Implementing Educational Practices Supported by Rigorous Evidence: A User-Friendly Guide." Washington, DC: U.S. Department of Education. www.excel-gov.org/evidence.

Eisner, E. 1991/1998. *The Enlightened Eye: Qualitative Inquiry and the Enhancement of Educational Practice*. Upper Saddle River, NJ: Prentice Hall (original work published in 1991).

Finley. S. 2005. "Arts-Based Inquiry: Performing Revolutionary Pedagogy." In *The Sage Handbook of Qualitative Research*, 681–93, N. Denzin and Y. Lincoln, eds. Thousand Oaks: Sage.

Greene, M. 1978. *Landscapes of Learning*. New York: Teachers College Press.

Kincheloe, J. 2005. *Critical Pedagogy Primer*. New York: Peter Lang.

Kozol, J. 2005. *The Shame of the Nation: The Restoration of Apartheid Schooling in America*. New York: Crown.

MacPherson, K. 2004. "Educators Voice Growing Concern That Schools Leaving Arts Behind." July 12. www.post-gazett.com.

Rabkin, N. 2004. *Putting the Arts in the Picture: Reframing Education in the 21st Century*. Chicago: Columbia College Chicago.

Taylor, P. (ed.) 1996. *Researching Drama and Arts Education: Paradigms and Possibilities*. London: Falmer Press.

Part I

Dance Education

Chapter 1

Evolving Modes of Assessing Dance: In Search of Transformative Dance Assessment

Edward C. Warburton

INTRODUCTION

In late 2003, as implementation of the U.S. No Child Left Behind educational act began in earnest, Michael Winerip (2003) wrote a *New York Times* article entitled "Trail of Clues Preceded New York Testing Fiasco." Mr. Winerip reported "serious mistakes" in the state's new testing program. The first "hard core" program to be approved under the new federal guidelines, New York State had two-thirds of students failing the Math A exam required for high school graduation. While the state faced ongoing investigations about test design and development, Mr. Winerip posed a more basic, but equally important question to state education authorities: what is—what should be—the aim of assessment and evaluation in our contemporary society?

The aim of assessment and evaluation in education is to improve learning. This central fact differs from traditional views in the United States of educational assessment and evaluation as a basis for promotion, grade reporting, tracking student achievement, or maintaining documentation systems required by law. For arts educators, this central fact is further obscured by tightly held traditions and beliefs about the nature of artistic behavior and purpose of schooling. In dance education, in particular, we are a field divided by stereotypes about what constitutes knowing in dance, who gets to participate, and how we should judge performances to be examples of having learned something. A comprehensive solution to dance assessment is as challenging to find today as a fair math test is in New York State.

Perhaps surprisingly, the issue of assessment in dance has rarely been considered from the perspective of promoting dance learning. The goal of this chapter is to redress this oversight by first reviewing past approaches and then reflecting on present challenges and possible directions. It should be noted that this chapter will adhere to working definitions of assessment and evaluation that are widely used, and not very controversial, but they are by no means universally accepted or used. *Assessment* is the systematic process of gathering evidence of what a learner can do. *Evaluation* is the ongoing process of making judgments and decisions based upon the interpretation of evidence gathered through assessment. Additionally, this chapter distinguishes between assessment and evaluation that focuses on individual learner performance and that which centers on the performance of groups of students. The former is used primarily for the guidance of students and their parents; the latter constitutes a measure of overall program effectiveness. I deal chiefly with the assessment of individual learner performance, although there are obvious implications for program evaluation.

CLUES TO CONTEMPORARY
APPROACHES IN DANCE

At the end of the twentieth century, politicians and pundits suggested that the currency of choice for the next century's growing "knowledge economy" would be *brainpower*, as defined by scientific and mathematical ability. In the United States, elementary and secondary schools increasingly track students by scholastic aptitude, and prestigious postsecondary institutions admit only the top students. The road from the playground to Harvard Yard may be long and arduous, but the path is clearly demarcated. A typical American adolescent receives several thousand hours of instruction in high school and spends several thousand more hours studying. Yet for those who wish to go to college, much of their fate is determined in the three or so hours it takes to complete the Scholastic Aptitude Test (SAT) or the American College Test (ACT). People who score well on these high-stakes tests will be granted admission to the best schools and, by extension, to the best access routes to professional success.

Traditionally, the arts have reinforced this ability-driven viewpoint. In dance, the currency of choice is *talent*, with a concept of the dancer as a special person, born with unique gifts. Great works or performances emerge effortlessly (or fail to emerge) and nothing anyone does will affect the outcome, as the story goes. There is no discernible relation between the cognitive or creative processes the dancer engages in and the final product. This folk belief in "talent will out" is reiterated in countless biographical accounts and personal anecdotes. A typical ode to talent is found in Greg Lawrence's (2001) biography of Jerome Robbins, which quotes Mimi Gomber as recalling that Robbins "knew where he was going and, of course, the talent came out" (50).

The belief in talent declares that unique abilities will flourish regardless of context or educational intervention. The key is to identify special children early so that they can hone their abilities and become truly exceptional. The conventional evaluation of talent in dance relies on highly subjective "one-shot" competitions or auditions where performance and product are the gold standards. Typically dancers are assembled like young calves at market and examiners rate them first by physical attributes. Dancers are then evaluated on a series of discrete tasks that require a wide range of skills, such as physical control and recall, coordination and agility, spatial awareness, rhythm, and musical phrasing. People who do well in these high-stakes auditions, which assess exclusively kinesthetic and musical abilities, are escorted into the rarefied world of professional dance.

Ideas about brainpower and talent stem from a long history in the United States of identifying gifted persons for special training in the arts or sciences. Criticism of this approach has come from diverse quarters, but especially from contemporary psychologists and educators. Over the past three decades, these researchers and policy-makers have argued that educational paradigms that rely on general intellectual ability, or "g," and "talent-will-out" models overemphasize a small subset of the full range of human abilities. Such models employ narrowly defined assessment vehicles that limit individuals' opportunities to demonstrate a range of understandings. How can a single audition possibly evaluate a dancer's potential? How does one account for the combination of kinesthetic skills, intrapersonal (self) knowledge, and creativity that is required to practice, perfect, and perform a dance solo? These critics point to the fallacious belief that human competencies are (1) universally attained or so unique as to be in a category all their own, and (2) not susceptible to development over time as individuals gain culturally specific experiences and education. This bimodal, invariant notion of knowledge and skill development ignores the fact that what it means to become human depends heavily on environmental circumstances (Rogoff, 1990, 2003).

More recently, pluralistic theories of intelligence have opened new vistas on the nature of human development (Gardner, 1983; Guilford, 1967; Sternberg, 1988). The notion of a multiplicity of human intelligent performances suggests that it is not sufficient to be able simply to "know" or "do" the work of our chosen domain; instead, we must strive for deep understanding and be able to demonstrate it in multiple ways. This changing view of the structure of mind finds support in recent theories of cognitive development, especially those that emphasize individual development in discipline-based domains of knowledge (Feldman, 1994; Hirschfeld and Gelman, 1994).

The view that one needs to develop multiple abilities in order to succeed in scholastic or performing arts settings is remote from conceptions of human beings as smart or talented. For many, the best way to countermand the prevailing folk notions of intelligent performance is to devise assessment measures that reveal the "richness, multidimensionality, and diversity" in human behavior (Achter, Benbow, & Lubinski, 1997). The multidimensional perspective suggests that, in the arts, while production should be at the center of the artistic experience, *understanding* requires the ability to adopt different stances toward the work (Gardner, 1991). The ability to approach the work from the stance of an audience member, critic, performer, and maker, among others, is crucial to the development of knowledge in the domain.

TOWARD MULTIDIMENSIONAL ASSESSMENT

The multidimensional perspective calls for "intelligence-fair" assessments that encompass all the individual's cognitive abilities, explicitly avoiding the measurement of an individual's mettle through the window of isolated abilities. Intelligence-fair assessment has two

requirements. First, assessment procedures should be contextual-
ized or "authentic." Individuals must be assessed in situations that
closely parallel conditions typical of the domain. For example, the
best assessment of a lawyer's ability would focus on the activities
that practitioners in this domain actually do (for example, briefing
a case or interacting with clients). In the performing arts, this
requirement seems almost trite. The nature of the arts requires
assessments that are performance-based. But innovators of authentic assessment focus on what students actually understand about the
subjects they learn and if they can demonstrate their understanding
in performance (doing) with comprehension (explaining) (Baron
and Wolf, 1996; Darling-Hammond, Ancess, and Falk, 1995; Wolf,
Bixby, Glenn, and Gardner, 1991). In dance, learners more often
demonstrate their learning by doing dance than they do by explaining it.

The second requirement calls for intelligence-fair assessments
that are by definition *ongoing*—that is, structured with repeated data
collection events—as opposed to the one-shot variety. This provision runs counter to conventional "audition" practices in dance.
Even if an audition could be devised to capture everything about
the dancer's abilities, a single test-administration could not capture
long-term aspects of the target performance (for instance, degree of
motivation, ability to bring difficult projects to fruition). A true
assessment can be made only by evaluating the individual over
time, using multiple measures. Dance companies the world over
know this to be true, and in fact assign plum roles based on such
information, but they also remain as committed to one-shot-deal
tests of ability as most U.S. colleges and universities are devoted to
the SAT and ACT.

For dance educators in the United States, these societal theories
of mind and evaluation practices underscore historical differences
between "educational" and "professional" curricular models. Two
models that continue to drive many programs in our public and private elementary and secondary (K–12) schools.[1] The educational
model derives its main precepts largely from Rudolf Laban's (1948)
treatise *Modern Educational Dance*. Laban viewed dance as contributing to the learner's overall development as a moving/feeling being.
The focus is on a meaningful process guided by a set of principles
about movement rather than on stylistically defined techniques.
Dance educators who work in this mode are primarily at the elementary level. They emphasize development of creativity, imagination,

subjectivity, and a problem-solving approach. In contrast, the professional model influences much of dance in secondary schools (and all levels in most private dance studios). Its main purpose is to train highly skilled dancers and produce theatrically defined dances for presentation. The curriculum deals mainly with the acquisition of dance technique, and occasionally compositional skills, with little time for creative or conceptual work.

When considering the merits of these opposing models of dance education in terms of assessment and evaluation, it becomes clear that both have practical and philosophical problems. The educational model respects the pluralistic mode of being and is inherently "intelligence fair": the focus is on the formative assessment of a range of abilities over time. On closer inspection, however, one finds the core of Laban's moving/feeling experience is impossible to evaluate. If one is concerned about the acquisition and retention of disciplinary knowledge, then no matter how good the process feels to young dancers there must be some reflection on what has been produced in order to guide aesthetic growth and understanding. The professional model, on the other hand, adheres to a particular kind of physical education approach; it provides ample opportunity to assess young dancers since specific physical and technical criteria can be isolated and quantified. However, this model makes no apology for emphasizing the final product, with mimicry of set work and little to no attention paid to cognitive or emotional engagement in creative performance or choreography. The discrete skill focus and single summative evaluation are clearly noneducational.

Over the past several decades, a number of visual and performing arts educators in the United States and abroad have sought to bridge educational and professional models with a blending of different assessment dimensions, practices, and purposes. A third curricular model, generally known as the "dance as art" approach, has grown in influence. It emphasizes both the quality of the experience and of the product that results from that experience. Jacqueline Smith-Autard's (1994) "midway model" is a well-known theoretical foundation for the integration of process- and product-oriented approaches. Smith-Autard's comprehensive model incorporates the flexibility of Laban's so-called "open concepts" in movement with stylized techniques common in the professional dance world. Her midway model places equal emphasis on dance problem-solving and training through the processes of creating, performing, and appreciating dance. It is important to note that, while dance educators have largely embraced this integrated notion, only a few dance researchers and educators have begun to grapple with assessment issues related to dance as diverse aesthetic and cultural practices. These issues are discussed later.

Initially, the urge to integrate seemed to emanate from institutions of higher education, where university and college dance students showed a strong desire for greater articulation between educational and professional dance worlds, both in training and evaluation (Hagood, 2000). In the United States, for example, the first dance major in higher education (1926) found its place in physical education (PE) programs; until the early 1970s, most university dance programs were affiliated with women's PE programs. Later, dance transferred to newly created schools and colleges of the arts, effectively uncoupling from the new coeducational programs in physical education resulting from the Title IX Act of 1972 and the Equal Educational Opportunity Act of 1974. From the mid-1970s through the 1980s, professional dance preparation and pedagogy changed dramatically in higher education. Increasingly, as postsecondary dance programs came to view their role as educating a technically proficient dancer, the language of integrated dance practices and multidimensional assessment began to seep into the lexicon of dance in higher education.

By the late 1980s, however, only a handful of dance educators in elementary, secondary, and postsecondary settings had embraced the tools of the nascent authentic assessment movement, such as rubrics, portfolios, process folios, and journals (Schmid, 2003). Eventually, both here and abroad, larger forces compelled dance educators at all levels to become involved in discussions of the purposes and prospects for dance in education: namely, the drive toward new national standards, curricula, and assessments. By most accounts (Bonbright, 1999), the standards movement in the United States encouraged dancers to return to key educational concerns: questions such as what constitutes knowing in dance (i.e., what should we assess), how does one learn in dance (i.e., how should we assess), and when in dance do we find examples of having learned something (i.e., when should we evaluate)? The next section reviews the outcomes of this struggle to articulate and agree on knowledge, reality, and value claims in dance.

DANCE STANDARDS AND ASSESSMENTS

For a growing number of dance educators across the globe, dance came out of the cold in the late 1980s. Having spent the better part of the century dancing far afield from mainstream education, key stakeholders from Australia to North America and the United Kingdom joined forces to support national and state initiatives in arts education. Because art and music had long histories of public school instruction, many educational commentators applauded these dancers, dance advocates, policy-makers, visionaries, dance teachers, and teacher educators for making history as they achieved national recognition for dance education. Though some viewed this new voice as the ultimate prize—a seat for dance at the general education roundtable—others openly worried about this new status. A mostly unspoken question lingered: what will all the sitting and thinking about standardized norms and achievement levels bring to dance and dance education?

What Was Achieved?

First and foremost, these initiatives brought attention to the value and import of dance and dance education internationally. As early as 1964 in the United States, for example, the National Council on the Arts in Education recommended that dance be recognized as an independent "arts-related" academic discipline of knowledge (as cited in Bonbright, 1999). In the United Kingdom, however, it was not until 1992 that dance was accorded a place in a national curriculum (Education Reform Act of 1988). It is an unfortunate fact that dance education became a statutory part of physical education in the earliest U.K. National Curriculum (1992); indeed, the Northern Examinations and Assessment Board (1993) initially categorized dance more as physical exercise than mental effort with concomitant outcome-based assessment models. But it is also true that, at long last, a national curriculum established a program of study that prescribed what *all* students should be able to know and do in dance. This stunning achievement articulated levels of dance knowledge, composition, performance, and appreciation heretofore unrecognized in any other general education system in the world (Ross, Radnor, Mitchell, and Bierton, 1993; Smith-Autard, 1994). Moreover, in the latest version of the general examination system, or General Certificate of Secondary Education (GCSE), a clear shift is evident toward viewing dance as an act of expression *and* intelligence (Assessment and Qualifications Alliance, 2000). The current schemes include criteria that assess dance understanding on a variety of dimensions and in much more nuanced and detailed ways.

While dance educators in the United Kingdom gained a foothold in the national curriculum, dance educators in the United States stepped up their campaign. First, they aligned with other arts areas to declare the arts equal to core curriculum areas (National Dance Association, 1988). Perhaps due in part to new pluralistic models of the mind, educators and policy-makers achieved a consensus view of the arts as representing forms of intelligent expression, as "expressing intelligence." One tangible result was the U.S. Department of Education's National Assessment Governing Board sponsorship of the first ever Arts Education Consensus Project in 1992.

Motivated by what would become "Goals 2000: Educate America Act of 1994," the Arts Education Consensus Project began an 18-month project to create arts assessment frameworks in an effort to assess arts instruction in U.S. public elementary and secondary schools. The project worked closely with the National Center for Education Statistics and the National Assessment of Educational Progress (NAEP) to identify objectives and develop assessments in dance in the fourth, eighth, and twelfth grades. NAEP field-tested the dance assessment for the fourth and eight grades in 1995 and planned for the twelfth grade in 1997. Ironically, an actual assessment of student performance in dance never materialized because the number of schools offering comprehensive dance education programs was not large enough to obtain a sample of students consistent with NAEP (1998) methodology purposes.

The Consensus Project led directly to inclusion of the arts in Goals 2000 and eventually to important new initiatives that raised public awareness and eventually resulted in federal, state, and local support for dance in K–12 education (Colwell, 1998). In material terms, the support included (1) a large federal grant to the National Dance Education Organization for a three-year study of research in dance education, (2) development of new state certification requirements for prospective and practicing teachers of dance (Bonbright, 2002), and (3) a growing consensus on what constitutes "dance" in K–12 education across the United States (Koff, 2000). Most commentators agree that much was achieved for dance and dance education in the 1990s.

What Was Overlooked?

As in the United Kingdom, the focus on assessment in dance marked a watershed moment for U.S. dance educators. The U.S. national standards were created at the same time as NAEP dance assessment frameworks, which addressed integrated aspects of dance and adhered to many of the requirements of intelligence-fair, authentic assessment. NAEP assessments included measurement frameworks that covered both content products (knowledge and skills) and artistic processes (creating, performing, and responding), using both paper-and-pencil and performance tasks. The tasks themselves are widely considered valid and reliable measurements of understanding in dance. (It is also important to note that NAEP was expressly designed to assess a national norm, so unlike No Child Left Behind, individuals were not tested on all tasks and were not ranked according to ability.) For example, the creating task for the twelfth grade gives pairs of students ten minutes to create a brief dance on the theme of metamorphosis, with specific requirements such as beginning with a still pose, developing movement using different shapes, levels, and movement types, and ending in a clear still pose. Using rubrics—essentially a 2×2 table that includes "dimensions" (the valued skills to be scored) and "indicators" (descriptions of excellent, good, fair, and poor performance on each dimension)—students are evaluated on the dimensions mentioned above as well as the use of space, movement flow, and composition.

While the GCSE and NAEP evince rigorous protocols, it is debatable whether the dance frameworks adhere too closely to traditional academic discipline's notions about what constitutes valid and reliable features of assessment and evaluation. Assessment specialists point to five distinct purposes of evaluation: (1) monitoring the progress of an individual or group; (2) diagnosing particular learning problems; (3) shaping learning outcomes and instructional strategies, (4) describing the performance of students for reporting purposes, and (5) categorizing individual or group performance. Most educators emphasize the analysis and restructuring of instructional strategies as particularly important in light of curricular goals and objectives. Yet, what most educators overlook is that these five purposes privilege external evaluation. The fact that U.K. and U.S. dance assessments are wholly aligned with these purposes raises concerns about the heavy reliance in dance on external evaluation, an overriding absolutist assumption, and the neglect of the ongoing, developmental aspects of learning movement.

External evaluation—whether it is in the form of anecdotal reports, class tests, large-scale assessments, observational narratives, or performance tasks rated by rubrics—all neglect the essential role of self-evaluation. Self-evaluation (or the interchangeable terms of self-appraisal or self-reflection) plays a central role in learning. Self-evaluation is a principal tool in cultivating what Shari Tishman (1995) has called *intellectual character*: it gives learners the self-author-ity to revise, enlarge, clarify, and improve their understandings of the issues, skills, and tasks they are studying. For young dancers, the focus on critical thinking and their learning processes will help them develop meta-cognitive awareness, to "self-adjust" and begin teach-ing themselves (Lavender, 1996; Torff and Warburton, in press). Teachers who employ student self-appraisal techniques also recognize that the results can help them evaluate overall student achievement (Henderson, 2001).

Self-evaluation exemplifies authentic forms of assessment (Warburton, 2003). Typical self-appraisal questions ask, what did I learn, what risks did I take, and what will I change? These kinds of questions reflect the highest level of assessment, *self-examination*, because they require one to judge personal strengths and weaknesses (Pitman, 1998). The questioning stance is essential in dance. Self-examination is necessary for gaining the self-confidence and auton-omy needed to accomplish high-level performance and creative work. Researchers who study self-appraisal report that self-assessment and self-evaluation techniques encourage students to become more goal-oriented and more responsible for their learning (Marienau and Fiddler, 1997; Palomba and Banta, 1999). Dancers in particular become more active listeners and more adept at giving and receiving constructive feedback than they were before using self-assessment (Alter, 2002; Levine, 1994).

Beyond issues of power and locus of control, most forms of exter-nal evaluation also have built-in *absolutist* assumptions. Belief in right/wrong answers tends to bias the content and form of assessment protocols. Many commentators argue on philosophical grounds that there is no absolute way of identifying and evaluating "what is dance" and what is "good" dance (Goodman, 1978). Quality in dance is relative to context, age and developmental factors, training and experience, and cultural norms and values. The challenge of standards-based assessments, which by definition rely heavily on external evaluation, is the almost inevitable prioritization of certain dance practices over others. In this way, national standardization can inadvertently work against individual and local community values in aesthetic production and response.

An alternative perspective holds that collaborative observation and analysis is a more effective and domain-specific way to examine dance, since all dance practices embody inherently communal experiences (Remer, 1996). In this view, the community of dance participants—students, teachers, specialists, artists, parents—all have a role in assessment. Together these dance community members can collaborate on definitions, criteria, and indicators of quality along a context-specific continuum. The activity is inherently educational as people observe each other, reflect on their perceptions, and attempt to reach consensus about judgments of merit and worth. The evaluations become trustworthy and credible (as opposed to valid and reliable) as members establish patterns of agreement over time (Remer, 2003).

A third related concern is the emphasis on summative versus formative evaluation in the assessment frameworks. By focusing on summative evaluation, the national assessments focus on benchmark or endpoint results. Like exams in other subject areas, these one-shot exams look (and feel) a lot like the traditional dance audition. For many students and teachers, the tests can act as a kind of fright-inducing appendage to the learning process. In contrast, intelligence-fair assessments are by definition *ongoing*, capturing long-term aspects of understanding. They are not one-shot evaluations every year or even every few years. As is true in all subject areas, the GCSE and NAEP frameworks for dance focus primarily on a single instance of understanding, neglecting an important aspect of authentic assessment: the *development* of understanding.

Systematic formative assessment and evaluation, on the other hand, provide ongoing feedback to both learner and educator. One approach in dance has been to redefine instruction as "assessment-based teaching," where assessment becomes an integral part of daily classroom practice (Gringasso, 2003). Assessment-based teaching is characterized by teacher and student participation in the assessment and evaluation process. The teacher makes assessment an explicit learning objective, with instructional activities geared towards understanding assessment goals and strategies. Students participate in defining the breadth and depth of the domain to be assessed, and they regularly engage in self-and peer-evaluation sessions. By expanding the idea of assessment to account for who gets to participate—and how and when a community of dancers reviews its work—the hierarchical, external nature of evaluation is effectively flattened and made internal.

ISSUES IN DANCE ASSESSMENT

The foregoing discussion suggests that, while assessment in dance has begun to bridge educational and professional concerns with authentic and intelligence-fair approaches, there remain a number of unresolved concerns, conflicts, and considerations unique to dance. This final section considers how these issues manifest in the dance studio classroom and outlines some new directions for assessment in dance.

Visible Bodies, Hidden Assessments

Recently, I have begun to investigate the nature of dance teacher beliefs and the ways external evaluation—with its implicit, absolutist assumptions—influences instructional approaches. The research is situated theoretically in the notion of the "hidden curriculum": the idea that teachers teach much more than what is explicitly presented in the curriculum. The idea of a hidden curriculum finds its most comprehensive statements in Paulo Freire's and Henry Giroux's work on the sociopolitics of education (Freire, 1983, 1985; Giroux, 1981; Giroux and Purpel, 1983). It seems to be appreciated so widely that it is considered standard educational wisdom. So obvious that, judging from the recent *Handbook of Research on Teaching* (Richardson, 2001), a dwindling number of researchers consider the implications of teacher expectations or the ways in which sociopolitical agendas infuse daily lessons.

One line of investigation in the hidden *implicit* realm that has remained robust, however, is the study of teacher beliefs (Richardson and Placier, 2002). Teachers' beliefs have been shown to influence the ways teachers structure tasks and interact with learners (Anning, 1988; Richardson, 1996; Wilson, 1996). There is broad consensus among teacher educators concerning the nature and development of teachers' beliefs about learning and teaching (Brookhart and Freeman, 1992; Calderhead, 1996; Fang, 1996). Lately, increased attention has been paid to factors that influence teachers' beliefs concerning appropriate use of critical thinking: cognitive skills and strategies that are purposeful, reasoned, goal-directed, and presage critical self-appraisal. Recent research in particular focuses on the extent to which classroom use of critical thinking depends on teachers' perception of learners as high-advantage or low-advantage, that is, able, knowledgeable, and motivated (Zohar, Degani, and Vaakin, 2001).

The research on teacher beliefs is especially relevant to dance education not only because of concerns about external evaluations and hidden curricula, but also because of ideas about the role "hidden assessments" play in evaluating who gets to participate in dance and how they will be taught. There are many anecdotal accounts of student dancers who experience the dispiriting effects of stereotypical thinking about "who" should be a dancer, what they should "look like," and which dance styles are considered "legitimate" (Markus, Silva, and Windish, 2003). Such naïve beliefs about race, body type, and privilege pervade dance studio classrooms. Most often dance teacher beliefs are hidden behind audition or casting selections of the "best" young dancers; other times, such beliefs manifest in teachers' approach in the dance studio classroom. This latter manifestation is more insidious, since the studio is ostensibly where all dancers ought to be afforded equal opportunity to develop their skills and abilities.

In a recent study, I examined the degree to which teacher beliefs, and by extension their "hidden assessments," in dance influenced instructional approaches. I investigated practicing dance teachers' beliefs about the usefulness of critical-thinking activities in the dance studio classroom (Torff and Warburton, in press; Warburton, 2004). I found a pervasive "advantage effect": the notion that dance teachers' beliefs about effective use of critical thinking are associated with their perceptions of dancers' advantage level. When dance teachers evaluated dancers to be high-advantage—high in motivation, knowledge, and ability—they were more likely to favor high critical-thinking activities, such as self-guided work, exploration, discussion, and reflection. Conversely, when dancers were judged to be low-advantage, critical-thinking activities were thought to be ineffective and were unlikely to be used.

This study also showed that such beliefs gave high-advantage dancers a more absolute advantage than previously thought (Warburton and Torff, 2005). I found significant and pervasive beliefs among practicing dance teachers that (1) any kind of pedagogy—be it critical-thinking-rich or critical-thinking-lean instruction—is more effective with high-advantage learners, and (2) changes in pedagogical approach matter more for high-advantage than low-advantage learners. Taken together, teachers' belief in the efficacy of teaching high-advantage dancers, using more powerful pedagogical approaches, gave those dancers perceived to be high-achieving an "absolute advantage" over those perceived as low-achieving. Ultimately, this study showed that practicing dance teachers hold a robust preference for high-advantage dancers.

The finding that hidden assessments and absolute advantage effects influence instructional choices argues for an integrated *educational* and *professional* model, but only for those deemed at-promise for it. The absolute advantage effect highlights the self-fulfilling prophecy associated with such hidden assessments. High-advantage dancers, by virtue of being labeled as such, receive critical-thinking-rich teaching, which enhances their education sufficiently that future teachers are more likely to perceive them as advantaged and intervene with still more critical-thinking-rich instruction and self-evaluation assessments. Low-advantage dancers are subject to an opposite, downward spiral. Because they are perceived to be low-advantage, they receive few critical-thinking activities. This cycle will make it likely that future teachers will use only command-style lessons and external evaluation with them and inevitably will inhibit their artistic growth. Strikingly, the advantage effect enables the rich to get richer—to *know what it takes* to become a skilled and creative dance artist—while the poor get poorer.

Despite concerns about robust stereotypes and naïve beliefs, a number of innovative dance educators are introducing ideas, old and new, into the field. A cursory look at these perspectives might detect old battle lines redrawn between educational and professional approaches. On closer inspection, however, one finds concrete bridges and potential avenues for moving toward *transformative* assessment in dance, applying principles inherent in multidimensional, intelligence-fair, authentic, empowering, and transparent approaches to assessment and evaluation.

New Directions

Multiliteracies. As a graduate student at the Harvard Graduate School of Education in the 1990s, I recall vividly the first time the term *multiliteracies* entered the educational lexicon. A doctoral colleague who sat on the editorial board of the *Harvard Education Review* slapped down the recent issue in front of my breakfast saying, "This is our new wave." A group of leading educators from Australia, Britain, and the United States calling themselves *The New*

London Group had introduced the notion in an article entitled "A pedagogy of multiliteracies: Designing social futures" (1996).

At first, many of my colleagues assumed it was yet another application of the pluralistic models already mentioned (e.g., Howard Gardner's work in particular) or a recapitulation of the emerging *media literacy* movement, but this was no recapitulation of old ideas. The New London Group coined the term *multiliteracies* and in so doing extended Elliot Eisner's (1982; 1994) view of literacy that goes beyond verbal and numerical skills. Later in an edited volume (Cope and Kalantzis, 2000), the Group provided a more thorough-going discussion of multiliteracies that bridge cognitive, cultural, social and political concerns. By moving beyond *mere* literacy, which is the traditional system based on mastering sound-letter association, *multiliteracies* embraces "increasingly important ... modes of meaning other than Linguistic, including Visual Meanings (images, page layouts, screen formats); Audio Meanings (music, sound effects); Gestural Meanings (body language, sensuality); Spatial Meanings (the meanings of environmental spaces, architectural spaces) and Multimodal Meanings" (2000, p. 80).

A number of dance educators have embraced this perspective, extending its main tenets into dance (Gringasso, 2003; Hong-Joe, 2000). In many respects, the idea of multiliteracies is consonant with the educational approach to dance education. It has clear connections to multidimensional assessment. In other respects, however, the multiliteracies perspective evokes (and argues for) a postmodern and critical pedagogic approach, where transformative educational practices includes consideration of power relations, diversity of voices, and locus of control (Doll, 1993; Leistyna, Woodrum, and Sherblomn, 1996). Clearly, in curricular terms, a multiliteracies approach takes dance beyond Laban-based notions of dance literacy, such as motif writing or the Language of Dance (LOD) approach (Bucek, 1998; Warburton, 2000). It is also distinct from other popular models of arts education, like the Getty Center's *Discipline-based Arts Education* (DBAE), which focuses on the range of learner's stances toward the art form—as an audience member, critic, performer, and maker among others (Eisner, 1988).

Dance education as developing dance literacy, in the multiliteracies sense, is conceived essentially as the development of knowledges and skills in performative, expressive and interpretative realms informed by a diversity of languages, discourses, practices, and contexts (Hong-Joe, 2002). The educational and professional bridge metaphor is thus exchanged for a kind of web that ties together dance practices, understandings, and experiences. The main critiques of this approach, as with most postmodern approaches to education, are that it "murders to dissect." First, the ideas and frameworks are viewed as untested and unworkable in practice, being too complex and distant from existing classroom instruction. Second, as with the DBAE and LOD methods, these approaches are criticized for asking learners to spend more time talking, writing, and thinking about art rather than physically doing it. Third, postmodern educational theorists tend to adopt existing flawed assessments, rather than propose new assessments, or they reject the notion of assessment and evaluation all together. Despite such misgivings, many contemporary dance educators view this enterprise as a promising, and intrinsically valuable, approach to dance education.

Motion Capture. A second line of inquiry has taken a radically different tack. Moving from the macro back to the micro unit of analysis, this research examines the ways new technologies can be used for assessing dance at the individual level. In an ongoing collaborative project, the Dance Education Program and the Center for Advanced Technology at New York University are developing new motion representations that attempt to capture important subtleties in human movement. The development of new representations for human motion analysis has direct implications for assessment and training of movement skill, that is, observable, goal-directed movement pattern(s). Such veridical three-dimensional representations of human movement would substantially improve the ability of a dancer (or dance teacher) to (a) provide individualized feedback, (b) identify personal movement issues or needs, (c) plan training or instructional strategies, (d) evaluate change over time, and (e) predict developmental outcomes or movement improvement.

Despite all advances in the capture process itself, however, investigators in human movement still lack appropriate computer representations. Indeed, the best character animations are still handcrafted by well-trained animators as seen in feature films by Pixar, Disney, DreamWorks, and other animation houses. Over the past century a school of traditional animation techniques has evolved—such as squash and stretch, arcing, follow-through—that are important to convey weight and intention. For dancers and movement researchers using motion capture, traditional animation techniques may anticipate important perceptual cues, but they do not reveal key features that convey unique "life-ness" of an individual movement signature. Unfortunately, at present, computer-generated animations of human movement also lack those idiosyncratic qualities with important subtleties getting diminished or lost in the process. Movement ends up looking rather artificial and robotic.

Our approach has been to treat this topic in a more general and more scientific way using Rudolf Laban's work in Labanotation and Laban Movement Analysis (LMA). Labanotation provides a comprehensive quantitative analysis of body part organization and spatial orientation. LMA utilizes the quantitative concepts of Labanotation but additionally addresses the more ephemeral, qualitative aspects of dynamics and subtleties of modalities of shape change. LMA emphasizes the perceptually important features in motion, that is, body, effort, shape, and space. In the context of this study it is important to have the tools of LMA, because it is the qualitative aspects of human motion that are proving the most illusive in developing motion capture technologies and animation software.

In assessment terms, an analytic tool based on LMA motion capture is important for identifying and describing patterns of movement expression that signify both cultural and personal styles. Understanding these elements helps one appreciate what human beings have in common and how each of us is unique. By extending this analytic framework to representations of movement in a variety of media including animation, we expect that the new motion representation will capture the life-ness and expressiveness that is very often lost in the previous computer-based representations. For example, an *LMA visualization tool* could employ the movement databank to enable the user (student, teacher, researcher) to work with different movement components—illustrating them, changing the intensities, creating new combinations and examples—for the purposes of movement skill assessment, training, and performance. The limitations of such an assessment tool span the theory and practice of dance education. Dance educators could view this as a tool for "building a better dancer," just as sports trainers use sophisticated tracking devices to improve athletes' performance. Dancers may view the tool as less a means than an end to improved movement skill, rather than viewing it as a way to develop deeper understanding of the larger dance literacy.

ASSESSMENT IN DANCE REVISITED

In this chapter, I have reviewed the past, present, and possibility of assessment in dance. I have pointed to a sound theoretical basis for multidimensional assessment in dance that is intelligent, fair, and authentic, and I have outlined how this approach was embraced during the national dance standards and assessments movement of the 1990s. I appreciated the political achievements and importance of this movement for dance, but also explored ways standardized assessment and evaluation might undermine effective dance curriculum and instruction. I explored the risks of letting the assessment tail-wag the curriculum dog; I argued that the advancement of external, absolutist assumptions about dance neglects the ongoing, developmental aspects of learning movement. I argued for moving toward *transformative* assessment in dance by applying principles inherent in multidimensional, intelligence-fair, authentic, empowering, and transparent assessment and evaluation.

I suggest that such transformative approaches to assessment in dance, if brought to fruition through reflective practice in the dance studio classroom, have the potential to locate assessment and evaluation as a rich, accessible, central feature in the learning process, rather than a forbidding, punitive, necessary evil. More challenging than the call for new assessment methods, perhaps, are the changes that these methods imply for dance and dance education. The implications of transformative assessment beg for a paradigm shift in dance education, both in general education (e.g., elementary and secondary schools) and in studio-based settings (i.e., private dance studios).

This shift would require, among other things, a renewed value for the young dancer as less a receptacle of collective wisdom, technical proficiency, and choreographic tradition and more a person engaged in mindful expressive movement, skill development, and creative inquiry. Whether that shift will ever occur on a large-scale basis is difficult to predict. One thing is certain, however: as our understandings of human intellectual and expressive potentials enlarge, as our appreciations for dance practices expand, and as our tools for charting human development improve, so too must we extend our vision and practice of dance and dance education.

NOTE

[1] Note that I refer mainly to dance education that includes multicultural forms of dance but which primarily focuses on dance as art form, sometimes referred to as theatrical dance, and not social or religious dance.

WORKS CITED

Achter, J. A., C. P. Benbow, and D. Lubinski. 1997. "Rethinking Multipotentiality Among the Intellectually Gifted: A Critical Review and Recommendations." *Gifted Child Quarterly,* 41, 13: 16.

Alter, J. B. 2002. "Self-appraisal and Pedagogical Practice: Performance-based Assessment Approaches." *Dance Research Journal,* 34(2): 79–92.

Anning, A. 1988. "Teachers' Theories About Children's Learning." In *Teachers Professional Learning.* J. Calderhead, ed. 128–45. London: Falmer Press.

Assessment and Qualifications Alliance. 2000. *General Certificate of Education, Performing Arts: Dance.* Adamsway, UK: Linneys ESL.

Baron, J. B., and D. P. Wolf (eds.) 1996. *Performance-based Student Assessment: Challenges and Possibilities.* Ninety-fifth Yearbook of the National Society for the Study of Education. Chicago, IL: University of Chicago Press.

Berliner, D. C., and R. C. Calfee (eds.) 1996. *Handbook of Educational Psychology.* New York: Macmillan.

Bonbright, J. M. 1999. "Dance Education 1999: Status, challenges, and Recommendations." *Arts Education Policy Review,* 101(1): 33–39.

———. 2002. "The Status of Dance Teacher Certification in the United States." *Journal of Dance Education,* 2(2): 63–67.

Brookhart, S., and D. Freeman. 1992. "Characteristics of Entering Teacher Candidates." *Review of Educational Research,* 62: 37–60.

Bucek, L. 1998. "Developing Dance Literacy: Integrating Motif Writing into Theme-based Children's Dance Classes." *Journal of Physical Education, Recreation and Dance,* 69(7): 29–32.

Calderhead, J. 1996. "Teachers: Beliefs and Knowledge." In *Handbook of Educational psychology.* D. C. Berliner and R. C. Calfee, eds. 709–25. New York: Macmillan.

Colwell, R. 1998. "Preparing Student Teachers in Assessment." *Arts Education Policy Review,* 99(4): 29–36.

Consortium of National Arts Education Associations. 1996. *Teacher Education for the Arts Disciplines: Issues Raised by the National Standards for Arts Education.* Washington, DC: Author.

Cope, B., and M. Kalantzis (eds.) 2000. *Multiliteracies: Literacy Learning and the Design of Social Futures.* London: Routledge.

Darling-Hammond, L., J. Ancess, J. and B. Falk. 1995. *Authentic Assessment in Action: Studies of Schools and Students at Work*. New York: Teachers College Press.

Doll, W. 1993. *A Postmodern Perspective on Curriculum*. New York: Teachers College Press.

Eisner, E. W. 1982. *Cognition and Curriculum: A Basis for Deciding What to Teach*. New York: Longman.

———. 1988. *The Role of Discipline-based Art Education in America's Schools*. Los Angeles, CA: Getty Center for Education in the Arts.

———. 1994. *Cognition and Curriculum Reconsidered* (2d ed.). New York: Teachers College Press.

Fang, Z. 1996. "A Review of Research on Teacher Beliefs and Practices." *Educational Research*, 38(1): 47–65.

Feldman, D. 1994. *Beyond Universals in Cognitive Development*. Norwood, NJ: Ablex Publishing.

Freire, P. 1983. *Pedagogy of the Oppressed*. New York: Continuum.

———. 1985. *The Politics of Education: Culture, Power, and Liberation*. New York: Bergin & Garvey.

Gardner, H. 1983. *Frames of Mind: The Theory of Multiple Intelligences*. New York: Basic Books.

———. 1991. *The Unschooled Mind: How Children Think and How Schools Should Teach*. New York: Basic Books.

Giroux, H. A. 1981. *Ideology, Culture, and the Process of Schooling*. Philadelphia, PA: Temple University Press.

Giroux, H. A., and D. E. Purpel. 1983. *The Hidden Curriculum and Moral Education: Deception or Discovery?* Berkeley, Calif.: McCutchan Pub. Corp.

Goodman, N. 1978. *Ways of World Making*. New York: Basic Books.

Gringasso, S. 2003. *A 21st Century Syllabus for a Modern Dance Technique Course*. Paper presented at the National Dance Education Organization, Albuquerque, NM.

Guilford, J. 1967. *The Nature of Human Intelligence*. New York: McGraw-Hill.

Hagood, T. 2000. *A History of Dance in American Higher Education: Dance and the American University*. Lewiston, NY: E. Mellen Press.

Henderson, J. 2001. *Reflective Teaching: Professional Artistry Through Inquiry* (3d ed.). Upper Saddle River, NJ: Merrill/Prentice Hall.

Hirschfeld, L., and S. Gelman. 1994. *Mapping the Mind: Domain-specificity in Cognition and Culture*. Cambridge: Cambridge University Press.

Hong-Joe, C. M. 2000. "Developing Dance Literacy in the Postmodern: An Approach to Curriculum." Paper presented at the Dancing in the Millenium, Washington, DC.

———. 2002. *Developing Dance Literacy in the Postmodern: An Approach to Curriculum*. Unpublished doctoral dissertation, Griffith University, Brisbane, QLD, Australia.

Koff, S. R. 2000. "Toward a Definition of Dance Education." *Childhood Education,* Fall: 27–31.

Laban, R. 1948. *Modern Educational Dance.* London: Macdonald and Evans.

Lavender, L. 1996. *Dancers Talking Dance: Critical Evaluation in the Choreography Class.* Champaign, IL: Human Kinetics.

Lawrence, G. 2001. *Dance with Demons: The Life of Jerome Robbins.* New York: Berkley Books.

Leistyna, P., A. Woodrum, and S. Sherblomn (eds.) 1996. *Breaking Free: The Transformative Power of Critical Pedagogy.* Cambridge, MA: Harvard Education Review.

Levine, M. N. 1994. *Widening the Circle: Towards a New Vision for Dance Education, A Report of the National Task Force on Dance Education.* Washington, DC: Dance/USA.

Marienau, C., and M. Fiddler. 1997. "Enhancing Your Career Through Self-assessment." *Journal of AHIMA,* 68(10): 30–33.

Markus, A., M. Silva, M. and K. Windish. 2003. *Concealing, Covering, Cowering: Hidden Assessmnent in Dance.* Paper presented at the Forum on Assessment in the Arts, New York University.

National Arts Education Associations. 1995. *National Standards for Arts Education: Dance, Music, Theatre, Visual Arts—What Every Young American Should Know and Be Able to Do in the Arts.* Reston, VA: National Arts Education Associations.

National Assessment of Educational Progress. 1998. *The NEAP Arts Education Framework, Field Test, and Assessment* (NCES 98-526). U.S. Department of Education, National Center for Education Statistics. Washington, DC: U.S. Government Printing Office.

National Curriculum Council. 1992. *Physical Education—Non-statuary Guidance.* London: NCC.

National Dance Association. 1988. *Dance Curriculum Guidelines K–12.* Reston, VA: National Dance Association.

———. 1996. *National Standards for Dance Education: What Every Young American Should Know and Be Able to Do in Dance.* Reston, VA: National Dance Association.

New London Group. 1996. "A Pedagogy of Multiliteracies: Designing Social Futures." *Harvard Education Review,* 66(1): 60–92.

Northern Examinations and Assessment Board. 1993. *Dance Syllabus.* London: GCSE.

Palomba, C. A., and T. W. Banta. 1999. *Assessment Essentials: Planning, Implementing, and Improving Assessment in Higher Education.* San Francisco: Jossey-Bass.

Pitman, W. 1998. *Learning the Arts in an Age of Uncertainty.* Ontario, Canada: Arts Education Council of Ontario.

Remer, J. 1996. *Beyond Enrichment.* New York: ACA Books.

————. 2003. "Student Achievement in Dance: Assessing Performance Quality in Context." Personal communication. New York City, April 15.

Richardson, V. 1996. "The Role of Attitudes and Beliefs in Learning to Teach." In *Handbook of Research in Teacher Education.* J. Sikula, ed. 2d ed., 102–19. New York: Macmillan.

————. (ed.) 2001. *Handbook of Research on Teaching* (4th ed.). Washington, DC: American Educational Research Association.

Richardson, V., and P. Placier. 2002. "Teacher Change." In *Handbook of Research on Teaching.* V. Richardson, ed. 4th ed., 905–47. Washington, DC: American Educational Research Association.

Rogoff, B. 1990. *Apprenticeship in Thinking: Cognitive Development in Social Context.* New York: Oxford University Press.

————. 2003. *The Cultural Nature of Human Development.* New York: Oxford University Press.

Ross, M., H. Radnor., S. Mitchell, and C. Bierton. 1993. *Assessment Achievement in the Arts.* Buckingham, UK: Open University Press.

Schmid, D. 2003. "Authentic Assessment in the Arts." *Journal of Dance Education,* 3(2), 65–73.

Smith-Autard, J. M. 1994. *The Art of Dance in Education.* London: A & C Black.

Sternberg, R. 1988. *Beyond IQ: The Triarchic Theory of Human Intelligence.* Cambridge: Cambridge University Press.

Tishman, S. 1995. "High-level Thinking, Ethics, and Intellectual Character." *Think,* October: 9–13.

Torff, B., and E. C. Warburton. In press. "Assessment of Teachers' Beliefs About Classroom Demand for Critical-thinking Activities." *Educational and Psychological Measurement.*

Warburton, E. C. 2000. "The Dance on Paper: The Effect of Notation-use on Learning and Development in Dance." *Research in Dance Education,* 1(2): 193–213.

————. 2003. "Intelligence Past, Present, and Possible: The Theory of Multiple Intelligences in Dance Education." *Journal of Dance Education,* 3(1): 7–15.

————. 2004. "Knowing What It Takes: The Effect of Perceived Learner Advantages on Dance Teachers' Use of Critical-thinking Activities." *Research in Dance Education,* 5(1): 67–80.

————. 2004. "Who Cares?: Teaching and Learning Care in Dance." *Journal of Dance Education,* 4(3): 88–96

Warburton, E. C., and B. Torff. 2005. "The Effect of Perceived Learner Advantages on Teachers' Beliefs About Critical-thinking Activities." *Journal of Teacher Education,* 56(1): 24–33.

Wilson, B. (ed.) 1996. *Constructivist Learning Environments: Case Studies in Instructional Design.* Englewood Cliffs, NJ: Educational Technology Publications.

Winerip, M. 2003. "Trail of Clues Preceded New York Testing Fiasco." *The New York Times*, October 15: B10.

Wolf, D., J. Bixby, J. Glenn, J. and H. Gardner. 1991. "To Use Their Minds Well: Investigating New Forms of Student Assessment." In *Review of Research in Education*. G. Grant, ed. Vol. 17: 31–74. Washington, DC: American Educational Research Association.

Zohar, A., A. Degani, and E. Vaakin. 2001. "Teachers' Beliefs about Low-achieving Students and Higher-order Thinking." *Teaching and Teacher Education*, 17(4): 469–85.

Chapter 2

Unlocking Dance and Assessment for Better Learning

Christina Hong

INTRODUCTION

Assessment and its relationship to curriculum and pedagogy in the arts has for some time been a topic that has garnered significant interest and debate across the international arts education community. Recent gatherings have targeted the arts and assessment as a key area of investigation. Examples of such forays include the 2003 Arts Assessment Forum hosted by the Steinhardt School of Education at New York University, and the Special Interest Group on Drama/Theatre Assessment at the IDEA Congress 2004, held at the University of Ottawa. As a contributor to both events I witnessed firsthand the degree to which arts educators across the globe struggle with the demands of assessment. Many are clearly frustrated by the current assessment approaches and expectations prescribed by their respective education systems. The question of whether to assess (or not), how much, when, and what should be assessed involve complex and pluralistic issues.

Warburton's review and charting of current and future directions in dance education assessment and evaluation (in Chapter 1) provide a useful springboard for further discussion. In responding to the chapter I intend to reinforce several notions that have been identified and provide some further clarification and exemplification. In particular, I intend to expand on the notions of (1) assessment to support learning and transformative dance education, and (2) the implications of dance literacies and assessment approaches that might underlie this. Further, I intend to situate this chapter largely within the educational context of dance education practices in Aotearoa, New Zealand.

TRANSFORMATIVE ASSESSMENT: ASSESSMENT TO SUPPORT LEARNING

Warburton's chapter highlights that it is deceptive to speak of "assessment" in singular terms. Assessment is undeniably multiple. Assessment, and particularly high-stake summative assessments, can and does contribute significantly to the determinations made in regard to student futures. Assessment informs and shapes the judgments of parents, teachers, and policy-makers. Assessment links the world of learning with the society beyond. Assessment, whether it is high- or low-stake, whether formative or summative, large or small in scale, does impact on students and their future learning. There is no such thing as a simple assessment of a student's practice of a discipline, or of a student's acquisition of knowledge in a discipline, or even of a student's awareness of acquiring such knowledge. Assessment is multiple—it is socially and contextually situated. It encompasses the whole work of learning in collaboration with the whole work of teaching.

This collaborative process, one that involves the learner *and* the teacher working together in tandem to create progress in learning is the core enterprise of assessment to support learning. I am making a differentiation here between assessment *of* learning, which is inherently summative and implemented for the purposes of grading and reporting, and assessment *for* learning, which is formative and implemented for the purposes of supporting students to move to the next step in the learning progression. It is the notion of assessment to support learning that I believe to be the key to unlocking quality learning in dance.

Assessment to support learning is also referred to as educational or educative assessment. Gipps (1994) identifies Glaser (1963) as the first to propose attention be given to "educational assessment." Gipps argues that a shift from assessment to *prove* learning to assessment to *improve* learning was signaled by Glaser's suggestion of a transition from norm to criterion-referenced assessment. Assessment that promotes learning is embedded in the social and cultural life of the classroom and is an interactive, dynamic, and collaborative activity integral and internal to the teaching and learning process. Characteristically this involves teachers sharing and negotiating learning goals with students; helping students to know and to recognize the outcomes and standards they are working towards; providing feedback that leads students to recognizing their next steps in the learning journey and how to take them. It involves students in self-assessment and is underpinned by the underlying assumption that every student can improve and therefore involves both teacher and students reviewing and reflecting on assessment data.

In similar terms, Torrance and Pryor (2001) differentiate between convergent and divergent assessment. In convergent assessment the aim is to find out *if* the learner knows, understands, or can do a pre-determined undertaking. It is characterized by detailed planning, and is generally accomplished by closed or pseudo-open questioning and tasks. On the other hand, divergent assessment emphasizes the learner's understanding rather than the agenda of the assessor. The aim is to discover *what* the learner knows, understands, and can do. It is characterized by less detailed planning, and the use of open questioning and open-ended tasks ideally situated within authentic contexts. The implications of divergent teacher assessment are that a constructivist view of learning is adopted with the intention to teach in the zone of proximal development (Vygotsky, 1986). As a result, assessment is seen as accomplished jointly by the teacher and the student, and orientated more to future development, rather than a measurement of past or current achievement. This implies that quality assessment criteria need to be communicated to students and discussed not only at the beginning of the task, but also reiterated by way of an ongoing dialogue with individuals and groups as tasks are pursued and various forms of drafting, both actual and metaphorical, ensue. Such ongoing dialogue is crucial to realizing "scaffolding" in action.

WHICH WAY FROM HERE?

Clearly then, the need for quality criteria assume, as previously stated, the identification of curriculum achievement objectives and from these, the articulation of learning outcomes. Achievement objectives should buoy the dance curriculum and give it purpose and direction.

Achievement objectives support the curriculum but this is not to imply that learning is singularly linear or that it follows one predefined trajectory. The ways in which we learn are multifarious and the journey taken in the process will reflect a multiplicity of ways and means. What is important is that a learning intention or objective is set so that the direction for reaching that particular signpost along the learning journey is established. Assessment is dependent on these as precursors. In the absence of well-articulated intentions and objectives for learning and an understanding of how learners might get there, we might as well be like Alice in her journey through Wonderland (Carroll, 2003):

> "Cheshire Puss," she began rather timidly. . . . "Would you please tell me which way I ought to go from here?"
> "That depends a good deal on where you want to get to," said the cat.
> "I don't much care where," said Alice.
> "Then it doesn't matter which way you go," said the cat. (66)

Like Alice, some arts educators have similarly tended to embark on serendipitous journeys, happy to follow their proverbial noses, not quite knowing where the next corner, pathway, or door might lead. Such protagonists get caught up, like Alice, in the adrenaline rush that variously manifests in the sheer joy and excitement of the adventure or its alternate, the flight-or-fight response. To know, or not to know, which way to go and how best to reach the journey's end has long been an arts teacher's dilemma. For some teachers, articulating objectives, outcomes, and assessments in the arts runs counter to what they perceive to be the expressed purposes of creative art making. How can students be encouraged to be self-directed, creative, and independent, and at the same time have content goals that require specific acquisition of knowledge? For others, achievement objectives, outcomes, and assessments are akin to the maps and blueprints for learning that chart the territory and point the directions for learning and teaching. If I (as teacher) don't know where I am going then how will I know when I get there? If you (as student) don't know where you are going then how will you know when you get there?

TRANSFORMATIVE DANCE EDUCATION: DANCE LITERACIES

As Warburton has discussed in some detail, the role of dance in schools over time has undergone some significant evolution. To put it bluntly, the function of dance in schools has shifted stereotypically from school "window-dressing" to one that is now increasingly recognized as adding educative value to the holistic knowledge, skills, and dispositions expected of students in the twenty-first century. Dance education in an increasing number of national school curricula and tertiary-level programs has outgrown the tenets of its initial aegis under physical education. Contemporary dance education from school through to graduate-level programs now embraces a more holistic discipline study and typically encompasses the areas of dance performance, choreography, critical analysis, and an investigation of sociocultural contexts both past and present. In relation to the school sector, New Zealand, like many other countries around the globe, has in recent years reevaluated the place and value of dance within the gambit of national curriculum reform.

The Arts in the New Zealand Curriculum (2000) mandates that "in years (grades) one–eight, students must study, and have opportunities to meet achievement objectives in, all four disciplines" (90) thereby instigating dance as compulsory core study (alongside drama, music, and the visual arts) for all students aged between five and fifteen years of age. Provision for students to take dance as an elective study is made available throughout the senior school years. Warburton refers to the development of a literacies approach as one of the more recent philosophical underpinnings to dance curriculum. This notion of "literacies" in each of the arts disciplines has been adopted as the central and unifying idea for the arts in the New Zealand curriculum. Literacies are developed in each discipline as students learn to use the particular visual, auditory, and kinesthetic signs and symbols of each discipline to convey and receive meaning. Dance literacy is concerned with facilitating student learning so as to develop an informed and critical understanding of dance as a form of expressive communication and its integral relationship to various cultures and contexts. As students develop literacy across the domains they become aware of the nature, purposes, and contexts of dance in its various forms. They develop experience in sharing dance with others in a range of dance forms, and develop understanding of how to shape dance as communication through the craft choreography. They come to understand the way in which social and cultural factors impact and are impacted by different dance forms, genres, and styles.

The implementation of the new arts curriculum has promulgated context specific research in the field. Substantial New Zealand–based research (Beals, Cameron, Hipkins, and Watson, 2003; Holland and O'Connor, 2004) that investigates the nature of arts learning and the impact of arts learning on the lives of students has been more systematically and vigorously pursued in recent years. The Ministry of Education–commissioned *Evaluation of Professional Development to Support the Arts in the New Zealand Curriculum* (2003) found that students felt they learned well in the arts not only because it was fun, but because they could work cooperatively, and there were many ways rather than one right way to solve creative problems. Further, students believed that learning in the arts impacted on their other subjects and their lives. For instance, it enabled them to develop empathy, to try new experiences and to think more deeply about their environment.

Beals et al. (2003) relate the feedback from "Lyn," a school principal who observed that the new arts curriculum had changed the way in which students learn in the arts: "Students are learning that although the arts are to be enjoyed, they also require discipline and perseverance. They are something you work at rather than just play with" (99). From a student perspective, ninth graders interviewed in the research explained that their experiences in dance had helped them to see personal meaning in other subjects. For example, after their exploration of the Iraqi war in dance and drama they began to study it in social studies. One student said, "We can see that studying the war isn't pointless. If we hadn't done it in dance and drama we wouldn't have our 'feelings' about it, like why we chose a particular point of view. We can put ourselves in other people's shoes" (103). This example serves to highlight the shift in focus that has ensued beyond that of rote learning steps and set dances and is beginning to enable students to interconnect their learning with other subjects and their lived lives.

Dance literacy in its various applications is about the practice of representation as a means of organizing, inscribing, and interpreting meaning. Human rationality uses many ways of knowing, thinking, and feeling. Dance education within a literacy model considers dance as part of a web of education that seeks to educate the whole person. Dance, the arts, the sciences, and the other subjects that comprise the school curriculum are not singularly independent and isolated branches of learning but are interconnected, and interrelated within an integrated web of learning. Dance as a way of knowing is one way (among many) in which our perceptions of the world are organized, communicated, understood, and judged.

TRANSFORMATIVE ASSESSMENT PRACTICES

If students are to engage in and with dance as a transformative practice then, as Warburton has stressed, this requires a significant shift in the ways and means by which we assess students. There is by implication a need to diversify the range of assessment tools beyond that of the traditional focus. What then are the implications for us as dance educators?

For a start, we need to take the mystery out of assessment and make it more transparent. Rather than assessment as something that is externally *done* to students we must engage with the student throughout the learning so that they are inside the learning process, not outside it. It is vital that we assess the learning, not merely the product. We should set tasks in a way that requires the student to *knowingly* explore and use certain skills or apply ideas in the full knowledge that the application of these certain skills and ideas fulfill the learning intentions for this particular study. We ask students to demonstrate their ability in multiple rather than singular modalities. This means that we ask students to communicate their thinking through movement and actions, drawing, role-play, concept mapping as well as through writing and oral reports. We observe and listen more acutely to our students as they describe and show their work and demonstrate their developing dance *literacy*— thinking and communicating in, through, and about the dance art form.

We should engage our students in self-assessment and collaborative or group assessment, thereby enhancing their ability to reflect in and on their learning. Such engagement is integral to transformative practice. Core to this undertaking is the need for students to be aware of the big picture in relation to their learning. In more traditional teaching and learning, students know some of the parts, rather than the whole, and have become accustomed to receiving classroom teaching as an arbitrary sequence of exercises with no overarching rationale. As Pennison (2004), reflecting on her three-semester-long implementation of self- and collaborative-assessment tools in the context of teaching project-based choreography, concludes:

> As a result of these efforts students became more aware of their own strengths and weakness, and took more responsibility for setting

and reaching higher goals in their work. An additional and unex-
pected benefit for me, as teacher, was the precise reframing of the
class content material that became evident with the helpful magni-
fying lens of assessment tools. (18)

When students are empowered to take responsibility for their
learning and are informed and are aware of the big picture, they
become more committed and more effective as learners. The
capacity of students to judge their own work is of fundamental
importance in learning. This capacity significantly changes the role
of the pupil as learner and the nature of the relationship between
teacher and student. In constructivist and transformative assessment models the teacher and the student share power and reduce
the hierarchical nature of the relationship between "expert" and
"apprentice."

NATIONAL EXEMPLARS: ENHANCING
QUALITY JUDGMENTS

The notion of "judging" or evaluating performed work in dance and
the other arts disciplines is often mooted as being problematic
because of the inherently subjective nature of the assessment. The
development of written criteria, particularly if these are written
together by the learner and the assessor, and then shared and cross-
moderated against others, will assist in describing what the expected
evidence outcomes might look like. Even so, written assessment criteria alone are not ideal. They are insufficient in providing the clarity of focus needed to enable teachers to provide focused formative
feedback to students. Nor are they sufficient in themselves to help
teachers make consistent and comparable judgments about students'
quality of performance for summative reporting purposes. They are
also inadequate for students to use as indicators in their self- and
peer-assessment practices.

When teachers (and their students) make qualitative judgments
intuitively without reference points or guidelines a number of problems, such as reliability, validity, and authenticity may occur that
lead to this information being less useful for assessment and reporting purposes. As Warburton notes in Chapter 1, "Quality in dance
is relative to context, age and developmental factors, training and
experience, and cultural norms and values." Teachers' judgments
are guided by their understanding of the long-term educational

outcomes signaled in achievement objectives. However, it is difficult to express progress and quality in words alone. While words are needed to describe criteria, audiovisual examples that have been developed and moderated to meet the common expectations of the user group are needed to demonstrate quality. The desire to make more explicit the quality quotient of assessment in dance and the arts has led to the development of exemplars as an educational strategy in several countries.

In New Zealand, national exemplars in each of the seven essential learning areas contribute to curriculum; pedagogical and assessment practices that clarify learning outcomes; and enhancing student learning and achievement. Exemplars are examples of student work that are annotated to illustrate learning, achievement, and quality in relation to curriculum levels. The development of exemplars will increase teachers' ability to make reliable and valid qualitative judgments that may be used for reporting purposes. These assessments provide reference points that will support teachers' professional judgments about the quality of their students' work.

The development and publication of dance exemplars (print, CD-ROM, and Web) have made the desired outcomes of learning more explicit by highlighting critical features of the student's work. Dance exemplars provide a basis for discussion about important qualities, aspects, or indicators of learning with students, teachers, and parents. Exemplars are also being used with students to draw students' attention to critical features of the work, help set specific and challenging goals, provide focused feedback to students that supports sustained learning conversations, and to assist students to understand what features to look for when peer and self-assessing. While exemplars will help signal the direction for learning, their effective use in supporting learning will depend on the interaction between teacher, learner, lesson content, and the wider learning environment.

TRANSFORMATIVE DANCE EDUCATION AND ASSESSMENT FOR LEARNING: BEYOND THE BLACK BOX

To return to the key idea that initiated this chapter, dance education in the twenty-first century has moved beyond the "black box" to include not only performative aspects, but emphasis on a broader range of dance literacy contexts. It is also increasingly embracing a transformative role. As dance educators, it is incumbent upon us to respond to these new imperatives and to the new opportunities and changing social needs of this century. Accordingly, we need to examine our practices carefully. This shift, as Warburton reminds us, is inevitably complex, and involves linkage between curriculum, assessment, and pedagogy:

> This shift would require, among other things, a renewed value for the young dancer as less a receptacle of collective wisdom, technical proficiency, and choreographic tradition and more a person engaged in mindful expressive movement, skill development, and creative inquiry.

Dance develops our minds, and expands the ways in which we can make public our own and others' ideas, feelings, beliefs, and values. In a constructivist and multiliteracies approach, dance education engages students in collaborative and open-ended inquiry. Students participate in constructing, monitoring, and reflecting on their own learning and performance in order to become self-monitoring and self-regulating.

Assessment that is explicitly designed to promote learning is a powerful tool for raising educational achievement and empowering lifelong learners. Assessment *for* learning is not merely a political solution to perceived problems over standards and accountability, but the very reason for assessment.

WORKS CITED

Beals, F., M. Cameron, R. Hipkins, and S. Watson. 2003. *An Evaluation of Professional Development to Support the Arts Curriculum in New Zealand.* Wellington: New Zealand Council for Educational Research.

Carroll, L. 2003 *Alice in Wonderland.* Bath, UK: Parragon Books. (Original work published 1865).

Gipps, C. 1994. *Beyond Testing: Towards a Theory of Educational Assessment.* London: Falmer Press.

Glaser, R. 1963. "Instructional technology and the measurement of learning outcomes: Some questions." *American Psychologist,* 18: 519–21

Holland, C., and P. O'Connor. 2004. *Like Writing off Paper: Report on Student Learning in the Arts.* Wellington, New Zealand: Ministry of Education.

Ministry of Education. 2000. *The Arts in the New Zealand Curriculum.* Wellington, New Zealand: Learning Media.

————. 2003. *The Dance Exemplars and Dance Matrix.* [Internet] www.tki.org.nz/r/assessment/exemplars/arts/dance.

Pennison, M. 2004. "From Both Sides: Assessment Benefits for Teacher and Student." *ArtsPraxis*, Special Focus: Assessment in Arts Education, 1:18–38.

Torrance, H., and J. Pryor. 2001. "Developing Formative Assessments in the Classroom: Using Action Research to Explore and Modify Theory." *British Educational Research Journal*, 27, 5: 615–31.

Vygotsky, L. 1986 *Thought and Language.* Cambridge, MA: Harvard University Press.

Part II

Music Education

Chapter 3

Music Education and Assessment: Issues and Suggestions

David J. Elliott

Educators today make an important distinction between two forms of assessment: *formative* and *summative*. One type of assessment requires music educators to give their students moment-to-moment *constructive* feedback about how well they are doing their musicing and listening. During the in-class and in-action processes of formative assessment, we use a variety of cues and languages to educate our students about the quality of their efforts in the moment. In other words, *formative* assessment casts music educators in the role of coaches: we *guide* our students by targeting their attention to key details of their musicing (i.e., performing, improvising, composing, arranging, and conducting), by adjusting their acts of musicing and listening, and by cuing them to reflect critically about their musical actions.

In contrast, *summative* assessment usually requires us to step back from our students' efforts in order to examine, test, judge, and otherwise reduce their musicing and listening to brief, fragmented tests of skills and facts that we can "describe" as numerical grades and/or brief verbal reports.

The tensions that accompany this long-standing dualism have intensified dramatically in recent years due to the increased use of summative assessment by politicians, policy-makers, and school administrators. In jurisdictions where testing has become an obsession, teachers and students spend most of their time preparing for "objective" tests that have little or nothing to do with significant learning, or "deep understanding," or learning-to-learn. Needless to say, the emotional consequences of high-pressure testing range from anxiety, to fear, to trauma, for students and teachers alike.

Indeed, this dualism (and its side effects) impacts different music educators in different ways: artistically, ethically, practically, emotionally, and so forth. For example, some music educators enjoy the privilege of working in schools where principals view formative and summative assessments as two complementary aspects of a much larger enterprise: the holistic, *educational* enterprise of the school. The emphasis in these schools is on individual student progress, intrinsic motivation, and self-growth. Thus, the administrators view and support music educators as trustworthy professionals who continuously work to improve their understandings of assessment and, therefore, evaluate their students' work ethically, with care, and in a fully educational manner.

Problematic situations occur when administrators decide (for a variety of political and personal reasons) to enforce strict forms of summative assessment on all subjects in a school. In these cases, music teaching begins to resemble the worst kinds of math and English teaching in which tiny bits of verbal knowledge and simplistic skills are "examined" out of their normal and natural contexts of use and enjoyment. Often, music educators in these circumstances surrender in fear or despair, or leave the profession for other fields (including community music schools, which allow them to teach music *musically*, without the many noneducational strictures and duties that come with schooling).

Summarizing to this point, it seems fair to say that while most teachers see assessment as a means of supporting their students' growth and development, many administrators, school boards, and test designers do not. The latter care more about using summative assessments to identify "failing" students and "failing" schools in order to determine state and local budgets.

Is it possible to reconcile these opposing mind-sets? Can we find satisfactory answers to this dilemma? I want to probe these questions from several perspectives. At the end of my discussion, I will offer my views on this dilemma based on several sources: my philosophies of education and music education; my practical teaching experiences; and the savvy of many elementary and secondary school music teachers I have consulted.

GETTING THE BIG PICTURE

I began this discussion by making a distinction between formative and summative assessment. In the process, I hinted at something deeper: formative assessment is usually educational; summative assessment is usually not. (I believe summative assessment could become educational if it was conceived and applied intelligently and ethically. But this is not possible at present, for reasons I explain now.)

Many scholars suggest that today's obsession with strict and narrow forms of summative assessment are part of a much larger sociocultural movement, called the educational reform movement, and also called the standards movement. At first glance, these labels have a positive ring. Who could possibly disagree with or oppose something called educational reform? But as we all know, first impressions can be very misleading, and simple slogans often hide complex agendas. I believe this is the case with today's notions of reform and standards. If we look beneath the surface, we begin to see that educational reform is mostly concerned with *training* students. Reformers are not concerned with *educating* our young people in the full-blooded sense of providing a *balanced* curriculum for the *whole* child.

This is the message that many savvy educational scholars, critics, and teachers have been shouting from the rooftops for the last decade. Sadly, too few parents, teachers, and administrators have been listening. Too few "get the big picture." Too few can see the forest because their gaze is fixed on the trees. Accordingly, the vast majority of parents and teachers (especially music teachers) fail to notice that the forest (American public schooling) is in serious danger of "going down in flames."

Richard Colwell (1995, 2004a, 2004b), one of today's most insightful scholars, penetrates the hypocrisy of educational reform, especially as it affects arts education. Colwell (2004a) emphasizes that educational reform is partly directed and powered by politicians and business leaders who put "marketplace capitalism" above all else. In other words, says Colwell, "marketplace educators" will fund schools and teachers if and only if teachers are preparing students "to compete successfully, not only for jobs in their own country so better products are made and grown, but with competitors throughout the world" (p. 18). Michael Apple (2001) agrees: "For all too many of the pundits, politicians, corporate leaders, and others, education *is* a business and should be treated no differently than any other business" (1–2).

Writing about the teaching and assessment of English today, Sarah Beck (2004) makes the same point when she avers that summative testing in English is being used to "promote an elite work force for a capitalist economy" and for "denigrating the professional judgment of teachers" (134). In support of her arguments she shows how test items from the English portion of the *Massachusetts Comprehensive Assessment System* (MCAS) limit what students are expected to understand about literary genres and narrow their opportunities for developing a broad repertoire of "proficiency with the cultural tools of written and spoken texts" (140). She continues: "When standardized assessments restrict students' opportunities to demonstrate their full capacity to respond to literature or write meaningful prose, how can English teachers ensure that their curricula and instruction are not similarly restrictive?" (142). James Lee (2002) agrees: "Mandated standards do not contribute to the goal of success for all, because they promote a test-preparation mentality anathema to professional judgments regarding how to best engage teacher-learner connections" (37).

Apple (2001) puts these themes in a broader context when he argues that while it is true that America's turn toward narrow curricula and high-stakes testing is rooted in the fear "of losing in international competition," this turn is also driven by a dread shared by many white, conservative, right-wing, American business leaders and politicians: the dread that "Western traditions" (e.g., the English language, Western religions, and so forth) will be overwhelmed and lost if people from Latin America, Asia, and other non-Western cultures succeed in the global marketplace. In short, America's turn toward narrow curricula and simplistic testing methods is a "rightward" turn. As Schmidt (1996) points out, conservative forces have been successful in taking control of American education by boiling it down to "white bread" issues of economic productivity, a so-called "return" to "higher values," and more "rigorous standards," all of which center on teaching conservative values via traditional Western subject matter and noncritical thinking. Indeed, to the extent that teachers and students are forced to spend more and more time on "preparing for the tests," less and less time is available for teaching and learning creatively and critically.

Furthermore, educational reform, standards, and NCLB (No Child Left Behind) have created a culture of fear and failure in many American schools, not a culture of learning and growth. Many teachers are teaching to the test; they are not teaching *students*. Some scholars even argue that the last thing educational reformers really want are thoughtful students with the abilities and dispositions to think critically and creatively. Indeed, if we examine the way high-stakes testing has transformed American schools into input-output "measurement factories," then it's plain to see that educational reform is about conformity and obedience. This movement is about producing future consumers who will purchase the goods and services they "believe" they need according to the values of the marketplace and the fashions it cycles and recycles for continuous, uncritical consumption. These are the goals of capitalism at its worst.

In the minds of marketplace educators and conservative politicians, summative assessment is the key to winning control of the American curriculum and, in the process, securing the long- and short-term values and interests of American business (Colwell, 2004a, 18). In other words, reformers are acting on a simple fact: what gets *tested* in schools is what gets *taught* in schools. In short, conservative business and political leaders want top-down control of American schools so they can control and *manage* the future of the marketplace and protect "traditional" American values. In contrast, "*educational* educators" want control of the curriculum for the purpose of providing all children with a *balanced* curriculum for their complete development, which includes students' academic, social, culture, physical, artistic, and emotional selves. As a long-standing "educational educator," John Goodlad (2000) challenges the ideology of Reform:

> Reform carries a nasty connotation of things and people gone wrong and needing to be done to by others who have the truth and know what is right. We should be ashamed of ourselves as educators for remaining silent when the word is used in connection with school improvement, but, worse, for building "reform" into the lexicon of our educational narratives. Out with it, forthwith! Renewal is the concept we need, with all its accompanying connotations of health, flow, continuity, self-realization, and mission in the sense of daily attention to means being simultaneously the satisfying realization of ends. (12)

STANDARDS

Central to any discussion of assessment is an examination of so-called standards. National standards have two aspects: *content* standards tell students and parents what students should know and be able to do; *achievement* standards inform students and parents about the level of competencies expected in each content area (Colwell, 1995, 7–8). Without a description of the forms of knowledge that a nation's school systems can and should provide, it is impossible to renew or improve anything, let alone plan for the future. The call to develop national standards for each subject can be traced back to the "reform rhetoric" of the *Nation at Risk* report of the 1980s (Schmidt, 1996). Since that time, each subject area has developed content standards on the assumption that each subject has a core set of skills, understandings, and/or competencies. Achievement standards have followed the development of content standards in every domain.

Needless to say, the development of standards has sparked controversy. On the broadest level, "there was no public debate in the US about the value of the selected basic subjects and whether these competencies fostered in these subjects resulted in the best mix for American-style democracy" (Colwell, 2004a, 19). On another level, subject specialists challenge the notion inherent in the term *standards* that each subject has a core set of competencies that can be measured "objectively." Also, the idea of content standards is so ambiguous that competing camps can easily manipulate the concept to suit their own agendas and/or accept or deny achievement standards as they wish. Indeed, how is it possible to develop any "measure of achievement" when there is no agreement among experts about a subject's core set of competencies?

In the domain of English, for example, a joint effort between the International Reading Association and the National Council of Teachers of English to develop English language standards went through three attempts before a final document emerged (Beck, 134). Even now, however, there is continuing and widespread disagreement in this domain (Mayher, 1999).

An even more basic problem with content and achievement standards is that they "do not begin to speak to the basic issues of equity in funding, opportunities, and quality among schools representing communities with vastly differing economic levels" (Schmidt, 73). In line with Elliot Eisner (1993), Colwell (1995) makes the same point in the form of a question: "How can one determine what a fair standard is when some students are hungry while others are indulged?" (8). Practically speaking, Theodore Sizer (1992) argues that the standards movement "will only prove that poor kids don't score as well as rich kids" (cited in Colwell, 1995, 8). In short, only after governments assist schools and support teachers in tangible ways can realistic standards be developed and applied fairly and rationally.

MUSIC EDUCATION AND STANDARDS

— LACK RELATION TO STATEMENT OF MUSICAL VALUES

Arts educators were the first to submit content standards to the Secretary of Education in March 1994. *The School Music Program: A New Vision* (1994) is music education's statement of content standards. This document was authored by a small group of like-minded colleagues at the top of the MENC—National Association for Music Education. The membership of the MENC was not consulted about the development of these standards. The membership had no opportunity to discuss or debate the larger issues involved in the so-called educational reform movement, or the relationships between reform and standards, let alone the details of the music standards themselves.

?

On one hand, we can understand the rush to submit standards and simplify the complexities of music teaching and learning for easy consumption by busy bureaucrats and administrators. *The School Music Program: A New Vision* (1994) has been successful to this extent. Music teachers can give this little document (and/or local curriculum variations on *The School Music Program*) to administrators and parents to "prove" that we are doing the same kinds of things as teachers in other subjects. The achievement standards for music "prove" (on paper, where it really counts to most administrators and parents) that music educators are testing students on atomistic skills and facts, just like all the other subjects. And, to the extent that content and achievement standards in music are not highly prescriptive, and to the degree that these standards are not taken too seriously by local administrators or teachers themselves, their official existence provides an "official cover" that frees good music teachers to get on with their excellent work according to their *own professional understandings and values*.

But the weaknesses of *The School Music Program* are obvious from several perspectives. The authors of the music standards simply "saluted" the dominant ideology of reform and did exactly what critical-thinking educators would/should have avoided: MENC leaders reduced the nature and values of music to a list of simply stated behaviors, and then outlined how teachers should measure these behaviors via simplistic summative assessment statements. In short, music standards were developed "with apparently little examination of the overall implications, issues or controversies" (Schmidt, 1996, 78). Put another way, a small clique of MENC authors plowed ahead on their own with the result that "the completed national standards in music represent and reflect the assumptions underlying the over-all standards movement" (Schmidt, 77).

Indeed, and although it is very possible that the authors of *The School Music Program* had sincere motives, it is fair to say that the preparation of this document occurred without the "big picture" in mind. In this sense, their effort was misguided. By jumping into bed with the educational reform movement, the leadership of MENC compromised the integrity of music, education, and music education. What I mean by this is that the national standards movement represents conformity and compliance with the most conservative forces in American culture today. In my view, music and music education should be free of (and resist) such strictures so music teaching can operate as a powerful force for individual creativity and empowerment.

But the kind of situation we find ourselves in today with standards is an old story, not a "new" vision. It's just the latest variation on an old theme: portray music as an academic subject (or a servant of the basics) in whatever formats and jargon the latest reform movement demands. (For example, in the 1950s it was behavioral objects and teaching machines; in the 1960s it was "concepts of the discipline," and so forth.) The underlying belief of our leaders is that if music educators jump on every new educational bandwagon, and comply with every new political manifesto, then music will be protected in the school curriculum because parents and administrators will see music *as* basic, too. Accordingly, our profession tends to operate *not* in relation to serious thinking, critical debate, and long-term planning, but in relation to a crisis-style "advocacy mind-set" that packages and repackages music to fit the latest ideology.

In any event, the national standards in music do not provide sufficient depth or clarity to direct music teaching and learning, or assessment. In fact, as one can see below, the notion of "music content standards" is nothing but a dry, bare-bones list of nine activities. *The School Music Program* is neither a philosophy, nor a curriculum, nor a pedagogy. This "new vision" is nothing more than a rudimentary list of things that people can do with or about music:

1. Singing, alone and with others, a varied repertoire of music.
2. Performing on instruments, alone and with others, a varied repertoire of music.
3. Improvising melodies, variations, and accompaniments.
4. Composing and arranging music within specified guidelines.

5. Reading and notating music.
6. Listening to, analyzing, and describing music.
7. Evaluating music and music performances.
8. Understanding relationships between music, the other arts, and disciplines outside the arts.
9. Understanding music in relation to history and culture.

Note, also, that because the music achievement standards are not related to any critically reasoned statement of musical values, and because they are not informed by any serious research, there is a serious danger that testing and judging children in relation to these achievement standards will drive a stake into the heart of what we want to develop most: our students' love of and engagement in music, and their intrinsic motivation to learn music, now and in the future. As Colwell (1995) says:

> The lack of serious thought about arts education policy ramifications is both striking and discouraging: ... Publishing the standards was premature, not only because in their incompleteness they fail to emphasize the individual human-ness of the arts, but also because there is no consensus on the meaning of *basic*. ... Policy debates should take place within specific philosophical and pedagogical viewpoints that give fashions in cultural and educational reform their just due but no more. (9–10)

What music educators need is not a nine-point list. What we need is a full-blown, critically reasoned concept of the nature and value of music and music education, including a concept of what musical understanding *is*. My perspective on these issues is called a "praxial" philosophy of music education (Elliott, 1995). Allow me to draw several points from this philosophy toward offering recommendations and drawing conclusions.

FOUNDATIONS FOR ASSESSMENT IN MUSIC EDUCATION

Music educators need clear "targets" for their assessments. To me, these targets include critically reasoned concepts of musical *values* and musical *knowledge*.

First, music and music education have many values. Developing students' musicianship and listenership through performing, improvising, composing, arranging, conducting, and listening enables students to participate in creating musical expressions of emotions, musical representations of people, places, and things, and musical expressions of cultural values. This range of opportunities for musical expression and creativity offers our students numerous ways of giving artistic-cultural form to their powers of feeling, thinking, knowing, valuing, evaluating, and believing, which, in turn, engage other listeners' emotions, interests, and understandings.

I wish to emphasize also that musical practices (musics, or style communities) are significant because the musical works they produce play important roles as unifying cultural artifacts. That is, cherished musical works are crucial to establishing, defining, delineating, and preserving a sense of community and self-identity within social groups. Musical pieces and musical practices constitute and are constituted by their social contexts.

Additionally, teaching and learning a variety of musics comprehensively (as music cultures) is an important form of multicultural education. Why? When good music teachers guide students as they "enter into" unfamiliar musics through active music making, students engage in self-reflections and personal reconstructions of their relationships, assumptions, and preferences about other people, other cultures, and other ways of thinking and valuing. Inducting learners into unfamiliar musical practices links the central values of music education to the broader goals of humanistic education.

By means of the above, students can achieve even more values: enjoyment (or "flow" experience), self-growth, self-knowledge (or constructive knowledge), and self-esteem (see Elliott, 1995, Chapter 5). How does this occur? As psychologist Mihalyi Csikszentmihalyi (1990) explains, when there is a *balance* or a *match* between (a) our musicianship (however naïve or advanced) and (b) the many levels of challenge involved in listening to or making music (as performers, improvisers, composers, arrangers, or conductors), humans can achieve enjoyment and self-knowledge. Formative assessment is critical here. Our students need our continuous feedback in order to understand when they are succeeding in their musicing and listening. Setting clear goals for their musicing and listening, and "telling" them (via many forms of gestures, cues, and so forth) how well they are doing, are central ways we foster and maintain their intrinsic motivation in music learning.

At this point I wish to link the values of music education to a broader portrait of educational values. In my view, the most essential, long-term task facing our profession involves enrolling parents, colleagues, administrators, politicians, and others in the quest to make our schools more *educational* in nature (Elliott, 1995, 306). By "educational" I mean that our schools should aim to develop students as *people*, not just marketplace job-fillers. As many philosophers have insisted in different words, *education is for life: education ought to be conceived for life as a whole*, not just for one aspect of life such as work, or schooling. Indeed, much more is involved in the full and beneficial "development" of children than "the acquisition of literacy" in the simple sense of "work skills" and academic knowledge, or the so-called basics. What more? Worldwide, human cultures past and present pursue a fairly common set of "life goals" or "life values": happiness, enjoyment, self-growth, self-knowledge, freedom, fellowship, and self-esteem, for oneself *and* for others. These life goals are so basic to human beings that people seldom ask, "Why do you want happiness, enjoyment, self-growth, wisdom, freedom, fellowship, and self-esteem?"

The major point I am making is this: *All school subjects, experiences, aims, and attainments ought to be conceived in terms of their relationship to life goals and life values*. Schooling should enable learners to achieve *life goals* in school and beyond school, in working life, family life, and social life. But if this is so, then music education should be in the core curriculum from kindergarten through secondary school because music education can enable all students to achieve the life goals of self-growth, self-knowledge, enjoyment, flow, and the happiness that can arise from being involved with others in musical ways of life. In other words, *music education is a unique and major source of many fundamental life goals*. By actively supporting the aims of music education, school systems increase the likelihood that students will learn to *make a life as well as a living* both inside and outside school.

Another issue concerns social diversity. Due to the multicultural nature of music as a diverse human practice, and because of the many kinds of social actions and transactions that take place during music teaching and learning, school music programs taught in line with a praxial philosophy can enable students to achieve self-identity, self-respect, and an acceptance of themselves and others. Since schools today are concerned with preparing students for life in pluralistic societies, and since schools themselves are more culturally diverse than ever, it stands to reason that schools should support the rich, cumulative, and enjoyable multicultural learning experiences that inhere in school music programs that induct

children into a variety of music cultures, as I suggest via the praxial philosophy (Elliott, 1995, 309).

MUSICAL UNDERSTANDING

Musical understanding is the key to achieving the values of music.
To me, musical understanding is a rich, multilayered form of knowing that is situated culturally, historically, and contextually. Musical
understanding includes what others and I call "cognitive emotions"
and "mindful feelings" that inform and guide the practical-cultural
actions of music listening and music making. In short, all forms of
music making (performing, improvising, composing, arranging,
and conducting) depend upon and express themselves as a multidimensional form of knowing called musical understanding that I
conceptualize as having two main aspects: *musicianship* and *listenership* (Elliott, 1995, 49–106).

Musicianship and listenership are two sides of the same cognitive
coin: that is, the knowings required to make the music of a particular style-practice (to perform, improvise, compose, arrange, or conduct a certain kind of music) are the same *types* of knowing required
to listen to that music. The names I give to these five kinds of knowing are procedural knowing, formal (or verbal) knowing, informal
(or experiential) knowing, impressionistic (or intuitive) knowing,
and supervisory (or meta-cognitive) musical knowing.

One way of "seeing" this model of musicianship is to hold your
hands in front of your face with your fingertips touching together.
Let each finger represent one of the five kinds of knowing. On your
right hand, you have the five kinds of knowing that make up musicianship; on your left hand, you have the five kinds of knowing that
make up listenership. Now interlace your fingers. As we develop a
student's ability to make and listen for a specific style of music, these
ten forms (fingers) of knowing grow and interweave, over time, like
your interlaced fingers. Teaching musical understanding means
empowering our students with a multidimensional form of cognitive-
affective-social-cultural knowing, which is unique to each musical
style they learn to make and listen *for*.

Allow me to offer one more thought about this concept of musical understanding. On one hand, what music educators do in
schools is the same as what all teachers do in the sense that we
develop our students' thinking and knowing. Teachers in every subject area focus on the outcomes of student thinking in relation to

domain-specific standards of accuracy, appropriateness, and origi-nality. However, what music educators do is unique because devel-oping musical understanding is a matter of teaching a multidimen-sional form of artistic-cultural thinking that is extraordinarily rich and, often, richer than many other kinds of "thinking" that schools attempt to teach (e.g., "teaching for the test").

RECOMMENDATIONS

In view of the above, let me suggest some ways of dealing with the narrow types of summative assessment being forced on us by the standards movement. First, it is essential to realize that our primary ethical and educational obligations are to our *students—not* to politi-cians, principals, state supervisors, and MENC policy-makers. Car-ing for the welfare for our students comes ahead of obeying the edicts of our bosses, if and when these people have their heads buried in reform and standards–think. Indeed, as I have pointed out above, many of our finest scholars offer many good reasons to believe that the standards-based notions being forced on today's schools by conservative policy-makers (powered by the legislation titled No Child Left Behind) are deeply and profoundly flawed.

If you agree, then I suggest it is important to make another impor-tant distinction between the *political* (standards) curriculum and the *practical* (everyday, working) curriculum. These are two different realities. As music educators, we need to focus on making our daily curriculum a humanistic, artistic, and caring experience for our stu-dents. Standards-based curricula are anathema to humanistic, artis-tic, and caring curricula because standards are driven by atomistic testing procedures. We need to be ethical-professional music educa-tors who make our choices in relation to critically reasoned concepts about education, musical values, and musical knowledge (*not* mar-ketplace notions of schools as input-output businesses). This is what excellent, qualified, *musical* music teachers have always done.

What this means in daily practice is two basic things: (a) we need to resist the pressure to employ rigid achievement standards in our daily work, because these devices are far too "bit by bit" to provide truly musical evaluations; (b) we need to protect the intrinsic moti-vation of our students by giving them continuous formative assess-ments in our daily teaching and, then, use these assessments as the basis for our summative assessments, which we should keep as gen-eral as possible.

In taking these steps, let us keep the following points in mind. For the sake of our students, our art, and our music programs, we will need to behave in two different ways that correspond to the two types of assessment we have been discussing here, and the two types of curricula we experience every day. Politically, and outwardly, most of us will be required to walk-the-walk and talk-the-talk of standards-this and standards-that (as long as this mentality lasts). But this does *not* mean that excellent music teachers have to apply standards-think in our classrooms. For one thing, the political curriculum is just a "paper monster." So, let us write down on paper whatever our supervisors require in whatever standards-speak they demand, then hand in the paper curriculum, and then close the classroom door and get on with what really matters: our humanistic, artistic, and caring efforts. The fact is that if we are teaching music well (in a caring, holistic, artistic, and humanistic way), then we are already exceeding any "standard" the writers of the MENC standards had in mind. Besides, the curriculum police (e.g., principals, or music supervisors) have their hands full. Thus, we will seldom have inspectors in our music classrooms looking for evidence that we are measuring our students by the standards. But even if they do appear, I suggest we simply tell them what they want to hear in the jargon *de jour* and then point out all the content standards we are "covering" in our lesson. (In fact, most well-conceived and well-taught music lessons that use even one or two excellent pieces of music will include a vast array of skills, understandings, and concepts that we can describe and teach in standards-speak). If this sounds too subversive, keep in mind (again) that acting professionally means caring for the growth and development of your students, not your inspectors.

As I said above, when we need to produce summative assessments of our students, I suggest we base these on formative assessments as much as possible. Formative assessments are not perfect (at all), but they are much more realistic and *knowledge-fair* than summative assessments. If necessary, we can translate the results of our formative assessments into summative assessments (and the language of achievement standards) by means of portfolio strategies.

[handwritten margin note: Lots of time + work!!!]

Third, it is very likely that the standards movement will fade and/or change into something different, sooner or later. Widespread anger at the huge number of failing students and failing schools caused by NCLB is already causing the government to reconsider its position. Indeed, I believe the severity of today's right-wing concept of "education" is a temporary phase. Examine the histories of American education and music education and you will see that we have experienced many swings of the pendulum. So, for now, we need to develop survival strategies with our colleagues (including those I suggest above) and persist with our central mission, like a stealth aircraft working under the radar.

Fourth, let us keep in mind that music is different from other subjects. Yes, musical understanding includes verbal knowledge, but musical understanding goes far, far beyond verbal facts; music is highly situational and procedural. Accordingly, musical understanding cannot be adequately tested or judged in the fragmentary, out-of-context ways that achievement standards demand. Moreover, it is essential to realize that, at the present time, we have no valid and reliable tests of musical understanding. As Colwell (2004b) emphasizes:

> Teachers need to be told, and often, that the focus of arts assessment is in the classroom, by the teacher, and that the external assessments produced by today's testing *madness* do not apply. State tests and the national assessment are not models for classroom testing, but just the opposite, for they do not provide immediate feedback, are not written in student language, and are not aligned with the instruction that has been conducted. (10)

CONCLUSION

At present, summative assessment in music education is a necessary evil. If we lived and worked in a more enlightened age and a more enlightened culture, then I am reasonably certain that assessment experts could create systems of summative assessment that would flow naturally from teachers' artistic-ethical-professional findings about each student's musical growth. Unfortunately, we do not live in such enlightened times. Today's educational policy-makers have lost their way. Their concept of education is weak. They are intent upon forcing all teachers and all subjects into one narrow mold. In doing so, they care *not* for the children or the programs that are being damaged and lost. This is especially so in arts education. Accordingly, and in the words of Neil Postman and Charles Weingartner (1969), I believe it is imperative that we conceptualize and practice *teaching* as a "*subversive activity*" (as I have outlined above), for the sake of our students and our art.

WORKS CITED

Apple, M. W. 2001. *Educating the "Right" Way: Markets, Standards, God, and Inequality*. New York: RoutledgeFalmer.

Beck, S. 2004. "Context, Text, and Tests: Issues in English Assessment in the United States." In *Teaching English Today: Advocating Change in the Secondary Curriculum*. B. Barrell, R. Hammett, et al., eds. 132–45. New York: Teachers College Press.

Colwell, R. 1995. "Will Voluntary National Standards Fix the Potholes of Arts Education?" *Arts Education Policy Review*, 96(5), 2–11.

———. 2004a. "Peek at an International Perspective on Assessment." In *Music Education Entering the 21st Century*. P. Shand, ed. 17–32. Nedlands, Western Australia: International Society for Music Education.

———. 2004b. "Evaluation in The Arts is Sheer Madness." *ArtsPraxis*, 1: 1–12.

Csikszentmihalyi, M. 1990. *Flow: The Psychology of Optimal Experience*. New York: Harper and Row.

Eisner, E. 1993. "Why Standards May Not Improve Schools." *Educational Leadership*, 50(5): 2–22.

Elliott, D. J. 1995. *Music Matters: A New Philosophy of Music Education*. New York: Oxford University Press.

Goodlad, J. I. 2000. "Educational Renewal and the Arts." *Arts Education Policy Review*, 101(4): 11–14.

Lee, J. O. 2002. "State vs. Local Control of Educational Standards." *Educational Forum*, 67 (Fall): 36–46.

Mayher, J. S. 1999. "Reflections on Standards and Standard Setting: An Insider/Outsider Perspective on the NCTE/IRA standards." *English Education*, 3(2): 106–21.

MENC. 1994. *The School Music Program: A New Vision*. Reston, VA: Music Educators National Conference.

Postman, N., and C. Weingartner. 1969. *Teaching as a Subversive Activity*. New York: Delacorte Press.

Schmidt, C. M. 1996. "Who Benefits?: Music Education and the National Standards." *Philosophy of Music Education Review*, 4(2): 71–82.

Sizer. T. 1992. "By All Measures: The Debate over Standards and Assessment." *Education Week*, 17 (June): 9–14.

Chapter 4

An Assessment of Assessment in Music

Richard Colwell

Portraying assessment issues through a *sturm und drang* scenario is confusing and perhaps counterproductive to the use of and improvement of evaluation strategies in music education. Admittedly, the use of a shock and awe strategy may appear to be the only mode that will awaken music educators from their "dogmatic slumber" about assessment and its potential. On the other hand, attacking is not likely to be successful because music educators believe, and rightly so, that they *continually* assess their important objectives and that they have other objectives for which assessment is inappropriate, time-consuming, or impossible. Both philosophers in music education and arts advocates often desire changes in the process or the content of evaluation in order to attract stronger support or political power, but I am not convinced that fundamental changes in evaluation and assessment practices are presently warranted *without* a thorough self-assessment giving full consideration to the important issues raised in the course of education's reform movement. Thus, this chapter attempts to build upon today's realities while accepting the need for reflection articulated by David Elliott in Chapter 3. One reality is that standards are critical in any field. Standards for health, the environment, or education are generally beneficial. A second reality is that standards can be misused and equated with standardization, high-stakes tests, and/or a narrow curriculum. A third reality is that the standards movement will open the floodgates to special interest groups or even to mediocrity within the profession by those who have only limited knowledge of the role standards can play in teaching and learning. Elliott's rich philosophical approach to assessment requires a lengthy review of realities as music education has developed multiple dimensions.

[margin handwritten note: WHAT THIS CHAPTER IS ABOUT]

DEFINITIONS

This chapter will not be a technical treatise about assessment, so I will not differentiate among measurement, evaluation, and assessment. Accountability, however, is a different concept, although the same data may be used, and is the focus of the public's present interest in assessment. Accountability suggests a shared responsibility between public and provider. In return for public support, an understandable documentation of results is required to demonstrate that the provider has, in all good faith, provided expected products and services. At the federal level, the GAO (general accounting office) was established in 1921 to provide unbiased documentation of the effectiveness of government programs. In July of 2004, the designation of GAO was changed to *government accountability* office to make the concept even clearer to the public. Linda Darling-Hammond (2004, 1050) lists areas of political, legal, bureaucratic, professional, and market accountability. One can understand how each of these is playing out in today's discussions—teachers of the arts want to be personally accountable and accountable to the art form while fulfilling any legal accountability that they have to their employers. The political accountability, which cannot be ignored, is a major issue especially when data are used to advance noneducational agendas (Ingram, et al. 2004, 1281–82). If the goal is to use classroom-based performance assessments for *accountability* purposes, then the indicators of quality must figure in the calculation, and they must be acceptably high. Such use of data (summative evaluation) restricts the flexible use of feedback to improve learning (Smithson, 2004, 215).

As Elliott suggests, the definition of musical competence for which the *school* is responsible must be crystal clear. Learning music and learning *about* music are aided by society's cultural and media institutions as well as by the family. A Gallup poll sponsored by the Music Products Association, based on 1005 telephone interviews, reported that thirty percent of the population of instrumentalists *PHILOS. MUST PRECEDE EVALUATION* learned to play an instrument through the school, twenty-six percent by private lessons, twenty-two percent by self-teaching, nine percent by being in a band or orchestra, and thirteen percent taught by a family member or a friend (NAMM, 2003). Elliott, how- *WHAT IS THIS? WHERE?* ever, seeks to delineate a new or better definition of music and a clarification of music as it is formally taught in the schools. For this effort, he is to be applauded. With assessment, clarity of purpose is all. A student's multiple encounters with music outside the classroom make any assessment with causal ramifications extremely complex. We need an "authentic" philosophy of music education before we can have "authentic" evaluation.

Elliott asks three important questions: (1) What is music? (2) What is musical knowledge? and (3) Why does music matter? I have elected to not wrestle with the first question as Roger Scruton (1997), a very conservative philosopher, tends to concur with Elliott, and their agreement on the first question is sufficient to proceed with issues in assessment. To understand music, Scruton stresses, one needs to know history and society's practices (456) and possess the ability to apply reflective judgment (459). He lists the following core experiences: composition, performance, making music together, making music for others, transcribing, arranging and embellishing, applying music to everyday life in dance, song, work, and worship, and listening (456). Elliot's attack on the study of *works* of art reminds me of a comment about British education that appeared in *The Economist* in July 2004: "After all, there is one thing worse than having an elite: not having one." Even given Elliot's and Scruton's accord, greater specificity would help. One does not need to be sick in order to get better. Reimer (2003, 266–67, 292), another important philosopher of music education, has also voiced a need for changes in evaluation practices; his product (as distinguished from process) priority is derived from musical criticism. The musically literate individual (a connoisseur) can make distinctions about music's craftsmanship, affective potentialities, imagination, and genuineness. In visual arts, Sabol (2004, 2) echoes Reimer, suggesting that competence includes the ability to recognize "use of the elements of art" and "overuse of ideas" (triteness).

In rejecting both superficial and fundamental suggested changes in assessment to make music learning similar to other "academic" subjects, I argue that what is known is not used, and that what is used is often inappropriately exercised and interpreted. My point is that our knowledge base is shallow and we lack the experience needed to make major changes in either our goals for music education or our modes of assessment. Elliott's concern about malfeasance in music education assessment practices has awakened me from *my* "dogmatic slumber" and I rise to respond.

HISTORY

Today's realities in assessment include the use of "high-stakes" assessments, assessments that determine whether a student graduates or is promoted. There is only a remote possibility that high-stakes assessment will ever be applied to the school music program but such testing in other subjects does affect the instructional resources available for teaching music. Most of the energy (and interest?) in assessment in music has historically been devoted to identifying *relative* talent. Students of evaluation recognize the contributions of Carl Seashore, Jacob Kwalwasser, Edwin Gordon, and Kai Karma and they may also recognize aptitude assessment "tools" promoted by companies that manufacture musical instruments.

Musical achievement has been measured almost exclusively by concerts, contests, and auditions; these are summative measures with moderate stakes. Contests use a semi-standardized "test" format as there is general agreement on what is to be judged. There appear to be only minor criticisms of these procedures. There have been three iterations of an external achievement examination, a music test as part of the National Assessment of Educational Progress, the first two of which were based on a consensus of objectives, the last based on objectives that were "possible" objectives derived from the 1994 voluntary national standards. A few states have constructed "trial" achievement tests, but of these, few if any have the psychometric or content qualities expected of a valid assessment. The known "models," if they can be so defined, for achievement tests in music are the Graduate Record Examination and Praxis Examinations, both published by the Educational Testing Service (ETS), and the National Board of Professional Teaching Standards (NBPTS) set of tasks. It is scary that our achievement emphasis has been only at this level, which could imply a narrow definition of music education.

PROGRAM EVALUATION

The literature in assessment is heavily weighted towards program assessment with its visible and direct link to accountability. The idea of students being accountable for their own learning, along with grade-level accountability and gain scores, is the most controversial component of the federal government's No Child Left Behind Act of 2001. My discussion of program evaluation is short because philosophers of music education, unfortunately, have failed to define music *programs*. The public can understand when a "program" is introduced to reduce drug abuse, to provide dental care for the impoverished, or to reduce obesity among America's youth. An instructional "program" might be designed to reduce the gaps in achievement among various ethnic groups within a school system or to increase the high school graduation rate. Familiar programs include DARE and Head Start, both programs that, at best, show only modest impact. (Bruner, 2004, 24; Magnuson, et al., 2004; Xue and Meisels, 2004).

Programs are often confused with curricula; for example, an intervention to improve the mathematical competency of all high school graduates consists primarily of a curriculum that could be constructed by an external provider. Success for All, Achieve, and Core Knowledge are examples of such programs. Evaluators not only can ascertain whether the claims for these programs are justified but, through goal-free evaluation, document unintended outcomes, positive and negative. Whether music education is comprised of "programs" of general, instrumental, and choral music is unclear. It might be that Suzuki, Kodaly, and Jump Right In are programs, as also are jazz or Advanced Placement Theory. Some may posit that the collection of voluntary national standards constitutes the music program, or that any experiences that can be defined as "making" music constitute the program and perhaps a curriculum. Do we have high school and elementary music programs? Must a program have a systematic scope and sequence for units, semesters, and a calendar year? I know of no respected attempt to identify and evaluate such music programs. Perhaps the only clear example of a program is the music education program that a student takes in college. If so, we have an example of program evaluation through the work of National Association of Schools of Music (NASM) and National Council for the Accreditation of Teacher Education (NCATE). Confronted with undefinable K–12 music programs, evaluators have not been able to draw upon any of the models of program evaluation that exist or models such as responsive evaluation, user-friendly, theory-based, utilization, and scads more evaluation schemata that differ primarily in the emphasis placed upon the various program participants in the evaluation strategy and the use and dissemination of results.

A FEW WORDS ABOUT ASSESSMENT

Our major source of knowledge about the benefits that occur from *use* of evaluation is common across the arts. The private music lesson is an experience in evaluation—one pays money to be assessed on tasks one has attempted to master. The feedback is immediate and very clear. The ensemble experience consists of striving for group goals such as balance, blend, and expressiveness, with the teacher (conductor) immediately changing (correcting) anything he or she perceives—the better teacher is usually the one who "hears" more and knows possible remedies for that which needs correcting. In both individual and group situations the goals are clear. Theatre and dance operate similarly and visual art instruction has long relied on a teacher who is able to walk about the classroom correcting and making suggestions to individual students engaged in creating art. Not one of these art forms has ventured into devising assessment schemata for outcomes beyond improved skill in performance. Music's assessment of skills has been a meld of summative and formative evaluation such as can be found in a dress rehearsal or, in theatre, opening off-Broadway. The assessment tool is observation and requires a skilled observer; Dorothy DeLay and Leonard Bernstein would both qualify. Thus, formative assessment, an assessment designed to improve both the process and the product, has focused on assuring excellence of the product—the concert or performance. Can we trust teacher judgments? Probably not, as Edwin Gordon (1967) found in establishing the validity of his *Musical Aptitude Profile*. Teachers believe, without concrete evidence, that most if not all of their students are making progress. Research data indicate that teachers give portfolios at least one mark higher than external evaluators (Gong and Reidy, 1996, 223). To improve observation, a common assessment, including the other arts, is the employment of an "external" teacher or judge(s) who also observes and then describes the performance as best she can through a rating scale and/or descriptions that teacher and student can understand. This mode of assessment has proved to be authentic, usable, quite reliable, and believed to possess multiple types of validity.

HIGH STAKES IN MUSIC

High-stakes assessment can have a place in the profession as long as the stakes do not depend upon one measure given at a single time. Single, high-stakes assessment, however, is an "authentic" part of some experiences in music. An audition for membership in an ensemble or admission to college is often based upon one "test" of someone's performing skill. Obtaining a teaching position can depend on a single interview. High-stakes test scores (multiple assessments) correlate well with teacher (or external) judgments and the error rate of misclassifying a student's true competence is fairly low. Only in the ideal world are judgments errorless.

STANDARDS

David Elliott rightly has a major concern with the voluntary national content standards (what musical knowledge is) and their impact on how music educators assess student achievement. Any discussion of the present voluntary national music standards requires more space than I've been allocated. The *standards* in core subjects that have emerged from the reform movement do not appear to be going away anytime in the future, although they are truly a product of the 1990s. Educators are presently stressing teacher/principal leadership qualities as a better way to improve student learning in a participatory democracy. The understanding and interpretation of the meaning of standards is much different in music from that in math, science, and language arts. I have been critical of the content standards as they were not presented as an initial draft, for discussion and reflection, or for their meaning for frameworks. There has been no attempt to establish priorities, and no endeavor to translate the standards into tasks, objectives, or experiences that teachers could use to incorporate new or neglected content into their curricula. Some teachers think they can teach directly from the standards. The music content standards are so idealistic that they actually provide no new guidance to the profession (except to broaden expectations). The public must wonder at the need to broaden the content when students presently are unable to accurately sing patriotic songs, including the national anthem. A better solution is to empower qualified teachers with the content of instruction. With few exceptions, present classroom activities (effective and ineffective) can be matched with one or

EMPOWER TEACHERS WITH CONTENT; NOT CONTENT "STANDARDS"
MORE, BETTER
(THEY'RE ALREADY "DOING" THE "STANDARDS" — AND THEY'RE NOT CHANGING WHAT THEY'RE DOING)

more of the content standards. On the other hand, publication of the content standards in the "core" subjects has resulted in considerable rethinking of daily and unit instructional objectives as the content is translated into teacher talk. As a result of formulating hundreds of outcomes (objectives) from the mathematical content standards, and with a decade of trial, mathematics content standards were revised and now provide grade-level guidance. Social studies standards have been controversial, modified by many states, and are now published for teachers in a voluminous three volumes. According to the Duluth *News Tribune* of May 18, 2004, Minnesota finally adopted their standards in social studies—in 77 pages!

Standards cover specific competencies that can be assessed. The assessment component is what differentiates standards from a goal or an aim. It is quite surprising that the individual states accepted the music (and the arts) standards without controversy or elaboration. The standards did broaden and provide an imprimatur for the array of possible content experiences based on composing; rap music; music integrated with other subjects—anything but noise. As evaluation must be closely tied with the intentions for student learning, broad standards can be misused as well as used. I sense a reaction by music educators that the standards for music do not indicate that music has a unique place in the curriculum. Thomas Popkewitz (2004) states, "The ways that children are talked about in research and policy literature do not vary significantly across school subjects. This is obvious in the curriculum standards of current school reforms. For instance, the national music curriculum standards are fundamentally about the child's ability to participate through informed decision making or problem solving, develop skill in communication (defending an argument, and working effectively in a group), produce high-quality work (acquiring and using information), and make connections with a community (acting as a responsible citizen)" (3). If Popkewitz represents most educators, there *is* nothing unique about music in the curriculum. Shulman's "Table of Learning," however, does suggest some commonality between music and education in the six waystations: engagement and motivation, knowledge and understanding, performance and action, reflection and critique, judgment and design, and commitment and identity. Each station, of course, must be interpreted for music and the multiple objectives possible in each stage identified (cited by Smith, 2004, 28–35). For example, critical thinking is frequently cited as a goal of music programs. Margaret Jorgensen says that the ability of teachers to frame thought-provoking questions is key to developing critical thinking in students; but this is not assessment, it is the essence of education—leading students to construct meaning (Jorgensen, 2004, 204). My point is that one cannot randomly add topics to the curriculum and still teach for understanding. Understanding implies coherence. The music standards omit only the ability to conduct a musical ensemble, an omission that is rectified where the need for a student to understand conducting gestures appears as a major competence in MENC's benchmarks for assessment (Lindeman, 2003, 31, 41). Debbie Meier (2000, 20) believes that the worst thing we can do is to turn teachers and schools into vehicles for implementing externally imposed standards.

The "official" standards are not those of the separate arts disciplines; the standards that were accepted by Secretary of Education Reilly are the five arts standards: the ability to communicate at a basic level in the four arts disciplines—dance, music, theatre, and the visual arts. This ability includes (1) knowledge and skills in the use of the basic vocabularies, materials, tools, techniques, and intellectual methods of each arts discipline; (2) the ability to communicate proficiently in at least one art form, including the ability to define and solve artistic problems with insight, reason, and technical proficiency; (3) the ability to understand and evaluate work in the various arts disciplines enabling one to develop and present basic analyses of works of art from structural, historical, and cultural perspectives, and from combinations of those perspectives (This standard includes the ability to understand and evaluate work in the various arts disciplines.); (4) an informed acquaintance with exemplary works of art from a variety of cultures and historical periods, and a basic understanding of historical development in the arts disciplines, across the arts as a whole, and within cultures; (5) the ability to relate various types of arts knowledge and skills within and across the arts disciplines. Mixing and matching competencies and understandings in art-making, history, and culture, and analysis in art and arts-related projects are expected. This set of five arts standards was translated into the nine music standards, an act that demonstrated the difficulty of translating arts policy goals to the discipline of music. Few music teachers are aware of the arts standards. Attaining competence in the music standards is no guarantee of competence in the standards for arts education. It should be obvious that the music standards written for pre-K–12 need further translation in order to serve as teaching objectives. The breadth (and vagueness?) of the arts standards was necessary to garner the support of not only all four arts but also arts advocates, education officials, and the public, without raising any opposition from arts teachers. Hence, a pond large enough to hold many fish.

The suggested content for music doesn't constitute a "standard" by any stretch of the imagination except that, by definition, standards imply assessment. Adopting standards for the arts, including music, may have been primarily a political act designed to gain support for arts education in the schools. The standards were to clarify for the public the outcomes that could be expected from "increased" support for arts education. Martella (2004, 13) suggests that the big problem in teaching is formulating *realistic* goals for what we are trying to accomplish. Missing that, the advocacy community has sought refuge in assessments that demonstrate higher achievement scores in other subjects, often mathematics and language arts, better school attendance, fewer dropouts, increased self-esteem—any bottom-line outcomes that might stem from participation in school-based arts. Arts advocates understand the need for bottom lines and accountability. The music profession does not appear to have been spurred to think about measurable musical outcomes of instruction and the development of valid ways of determining the extent to which any of these outcomes is being accomplished. As we do develop assessments, we must keep in mind that standards set high enough to exemplify truly outstanding work may be irrelevant because they are so far from current practice as to alienate or mystify most potential learners (Cohen, 1995, 754).

MENC CLARIFICATION

Though teachers may have been lulled into some sense of false security, MENC seems to recognize that the standards are not objectives. Mike Blakeslee (2004), deputy executive director of MENC, says that "it is time to apply to arts education the same clear goals for student achievement that we expect for other areas of the wider curriculum" (34). He also asks: What are the relative weights that should be applied to fostering student achievement in different standards? Should all nine be considered equal in importance? How do we proceed when music classes sometimes lack defined learning outcomes (32)? Good questions, all.

OTHER STANDARDS

With general agreement on the range of experiences in music, there has been no need for the profession to expend its cultural capital involving the public in verifying the content of music instruction. The needed standards are those never discussed: the proficiency standards, the opportunity to learn standards, the evaluation standards, and the standards for teachers. To its credit, the Music Educators National Conference did promptly respond to two of these critical standards. It published booklets on suggested proficiency standards simultaneously with the publishing of the content standards (MENC, 1994) and later issued opportunity to learn standards (1996).

OPPORTUNITY TO LEARN STANDARDS

Because both the content and the level of proficiency depend on whether students have been given an *opportunity to learn*, the opportunity to learn (OTL) standards are the most important. The profession did not need the assistance of advocates to promote the content standards; what was and is missing are the resources to attain minimum education in music. The nine music standards are infeasible without provision by the schools (and the public) for the opportunity to learn some or most of the "suggested" content. Opportunity to learn standards require resources of qualified instructors, adequate time, and facilities in which instruction is conducted. Opportunity to learn recognizes that a student can achieve only according to the resources available and the student's ability level. A few of these OTL standards (Consortium, 1995) for the elementary school include: (2) the curriculum is comprised of a balanced and sequential program of singing, playing instruments, listening to music, improvising and composing music, and moving to music. Also included are learning experiences designed to develop the ability to read music, use the notation and terminology of music, analyze and describe music, make informed evaluations concerning music, and understand music and music practices in relation to history and culture and to other disciplines in the curriculum. (5) Ninety minutes a week excluding elective instrumental or choral instruction. (9) General music includes instruction on at least two: recorder, fretted instruments, keyboard instruments, electronic instruments, instruments representing various cultures. (16) Special experiences are designed for gifted and talented students according to their abilities and interests (14–15).

Other OTL standards include:

Materials and Equipment. Every school has available microcomputers and appropriate music software including notation and sequencing software, printers, sufficient MIDI equipment, multiple electronic keyboards, synthesizers and computers equipped with CD-ROM drives, and music related CD-ROMs. Also available are video cameras, color monitors, stereo VCRs, and multimedia equipment combining digitized sound and music with graphics and text. Instruments provided include French horns, baritones, tubas, appropriately sized violas, cellos, double basses, and percussion equipment. Additional instruments are provided when students have difficulty purchasing instruments due to financial hardship. A repair budget is available equal to at least five percent of current replacement value (16–17).

Facilities require a general music room, an instrumental music room and storage (17).

Middle School. At least one year-long elective course in music other than band, orchestra, and chorus is offered in grade nine. At least one course with no prerequisites. Choral and instrumental ensembles and classes are offered during the school day and scheduled so that all members of each ensemble meet as a unit throughout the year. Provided are 15½-inch and 16-inch violas, ¾-size and full-size cellos, half-size and ¾-size double basses; C piccolos, bass clarinets, tenor saxophones, baritone saxophones, oboes, bassoons, double French horns, baritone horns, tubas, concert snare drums, pedal timpani, concert bass drums, crash cymbals, suspended cymbals, tambourines, triangles, xylophones or marimbas, orchestra bells, assorted percussion equipment, drum stands, movable percussion cabinets, tuba chairs, bass stools, conductor's stands, tuning devices, music folders, and chairs designed for music classes (20).

Every instrumental room has at least 2500 square feet of floor space with a ceiling at least twenty feet high and with running water; year-round temperature of 68–70 degrees, humidity between forty and fifty percent and an air-exchange rate double that of regular classrooms. Two rehearsal rooms have at least 350 square feet each for small ensembles; several practice rooms have at least fifty-five square feet each (21). There is stage lighting of 70 foot-candles; quiet and adequate mechanical and lighting systems that do not exceed NC20 (22).

THE PROFESSION'S UNDERSTANDING OF ASSESSMENT

What is unfortunate, although with the best of intent, is the recent publication by MENC—The National Association for Music Education of a wretched book on assessment under the strategies series (Lindeman, 2003). This publication provides examples of student responses at grades four, eight, and twelve for each of the standards. The editor states in the preface that *proficient* level should be attained by seventy-five percent of the class (ix). She also suggests that *basic* is different from *unacceptable* with the *basic* level to be attained by ninety percent of the class and *advanced* by twenty-five percent. How reasonable are these recommendations? Debbie Meier says that education is always about politics—in the best and worst senses. Meier states that "NCLB proposes to accomplish a statistical impossibility that all children score in the top twenty-fifth percentile" (Meier, 2004, 6). The Lindeman publication further affirms these impossible goals in the chapter by Brophy (2003, 12), who also suggests that the *proficient* level should be attained by at least seventy-five percent of the students and the *advanced* level by twenty-five percent. The misconceptions are so numerous that only a few can be cited here. The authors state, with respect to authentic assessment, that answering a question about instrument hand position is not authentic (xii). My impression has always been that one really knows a topic when one can teach that topic (hand position, for example) and *explain* it—quite authentic. If not, we would often be faced with only rote learning. The suggested portfolios hardly seem "authentic." The important and authentic evaluation is that of the teacher in the classroom, correcting, modeling, and providing feedback, employing primarily formative evaluation and an occasional summative task. Brophy (2003, 1) suggests that listening to an ensemble's sound and correcting it in rehearsal is an "informal" means of assessment. This assessment strategy should not be informal, it should be fair, comprehensive, and considered important by students and teacher. Well-developed ensemble skills for ages nine through twelve are to be assessed only by singing? When asked "What skills and knowledge are to be assessed?" the keyed answer is "all." Such suggestions are not only misleading but infeasible (2).

An important evaluation is assessing achievement of the performance standards. In the Lindeman publication, the suggested strategy is: "The repertoire performed should include at least three major instrumental works: works associated with at least four ethnic cultural, or national groups, and works representing at least four of the styles, periods, or categories of music typically associated with the type of ensemble of that repertoire" (38). *Advanced* level is performing music of grade four on a basis of 1–6 levels. *Proficient* level also uses music of grade four with the competence difference being in performing one fewer style and one less ethnicity (36). Basic proficiency also uses grade four music with the difference, again, only in the *amount* of music covered. There is no hint given that a performance, at any level, must be done well. Proficiency standards in music should be about quality, not quantity. It is better for students to perform grade three music precisely than to experience a sloppy performance of music that is too difficult. A reliance solely on description can lead to a focus on symptoms rather than cause (Anderson, 2003, 26). This suggested lack of curriculum alignment with the assessment supports the apocryphal distinction between musicians who teach and music educators. This publication provides a cogent reason for a vigorous approach by the profession to catch up with other subjects in our assessment competence.

My argument may differ from Elliott's in that I believe that multiple standards are essential to all instruction and that we do need content standards and a national discussion of them, which may result in seventy-seven pages or three volumes of attainable objectives derived from these standards. Anthony Palmer (2000, 106) argues that standards arise out of reductionist, positivist modes of thought, and function only on the first two levels of Bloom's taxonomy. Daniel Steiner (2004), Education Director of the National Endowment for the Arts believes that use of *even* these two levels would be an essential improvement (138). For Palmer, the standards have been instrumental in politicizing education. (Education was unfortunately scudding towards the political side of the fence long before the standards became a daily part of our lives.) The arts supervisor in Indiana (Brown, 2000, 118) takes issue with Palmer arguing that use of the arts standards which were "carefully adopted," energizes classes and that students respond positively to the clarity that the standards provide.

TEACHER AND TEACHER EDUCATION STANDARDS

My primary argument is that music education needs to begin with the known instead of flailing about, grasping ideas about assessment from a cornucopia of sources, none of which has been subjected to use in music education. What is known? One place to begin is with teacher assessment. As I suggested, our experience is based on the contributions of ETS, NBPTS, and NASM/NCATE. Changing college curricula (or that of the public schools) is not the way to begin until we can interpret, to our satisfaction, current evaluation data. We need to be able to define incompetence in teaching and to develop a few diagnostic tools. Self-assessment in skills is among the most difficult tasks: when skills are an important focus, self-assessment strategies will not add reliable information. Minimizing bad habits in skill development, even among professionals, requires the continuing feedback of a coach (weekly music lessons in conservatories) whether the skill being mastered and practiced is golf by Tiger Woods or basketball at Duke University. Music teachers use a one-way mirror in self-assessing—they can identify superior teaching but are unable to compare what they observe with their own teaching so as to lead to self-improvement. Any evaluation must be concerned with consequences, fairness, generalizability, content coverage, quality of content, and meaningfulness. One bit of data is missing and requires assistance from the research community: namely, there is no solid evidence about the causes of a program's effectiveness. Teacher competence is a probable component of an effective program. Although a number of authors have indicated that half of the teachers and administrators judge teacher effectiveness and school effectiveness by some indicator other than student achievement, present reform efforts are evoking a movement that will judge teachers based on student learning (Ingram, et al. 2004).

Teacher testing can be fruitless unless we know what we want in a teacher—a scholar, a performer, a leader, a counselor, a role model, or.... Assessing by student competencies would be difficult without grade-level expectations, and for grade-level competencies to be feasible there must be sequential instruction. Thus, the picture for one mode of approaching teacher evaluation is Delphic; before we initiate the process of developing teacher evaluation we must draw on our knowledge base in teacher education and in music education, as skimpy as it is. In written teacher examinations, the emphasis has been on music history and music theory, for these may be the only commonalities even though the teacher preparation emphasis is on performance, solo and ensemble. In the work on student assessment, curricular alignment with the table of specifications of any assessment is considered critical and is the major concern in high-stakes testing. Alignment is ignored in assessing music teachers—I've been unable to identify any state certification test, Praxis Examination, NBPTS task, or professional development that tests performance on major or minor instruments or reflects teacher training curricula.

TAKE A LOOK AT PRAXIS I & II

NASM has program assessment as a primary mission and has a long history of focusing on peer assessment, a rather subjective type and one that is usually considered more formative than summative. One can find few "standards" in the NASM evaluation documents (NASM, 2003). Within a framework of 120–124 hours, the "standards" for the music teacher curriculum are to consist of fifty percent studies in musicianship, thirty–thirty-five percent in general studies, and fifteen–twenty percent in professional education. Professional education is defined as philosophical and social foundations, educational psychology, special education, history of education, and student teaching. Methods and supplementary instruments may be counted as part of musicianship as long as the content is *primarily* music (italics mine) (94). One of the few competencies related to assessment is that "students are to be able to evaluate ideas, methods and policies in the arts, humanities and in arts education for impact on musical and cultural development of students and to evaluate correct ideas" (97). Another competency is an "understanding of evaluation techniques and ability to apply them in assessing both the musical progress of students and the objectives and procedures of the curriculum" (97). Administrators of the program are to use assessment to "provide an initial assessment for entry into the program, periodic assessments, and further assessment after graduation" (98). The other emphasis on evaluation is to occur in the graduate program where the recommendation is for one-third of the program to be devoted to the evaluation of research (107). If these recommendations were translated into practice, there might indeed be an interest in assessment, but NASM has no enforcement procedures for the music education curriculum and so these recommendations have not been acted upon.

The emphasis on music history and music theory in written tests can be justified in the lack of agreement on the music education competencies that may be subsumed under musicianship education or offered separately in colleges of education or music education departments. It is difficult to point the finger of responsibility for any music education competency. Accredited institutions Peabody and Westminster Choir College do not actually have the support of a college of education and on many campuses that do, students are not encouraged to enroll in courses taught by the College of Education. David Steiner, the new education director of the National Endowment of the Arts, wrote with Susan D. Rozen (2004) a summary of the competencies they derived from syllabi for pedagogical courses in foundations, reading, and methods required of all elementary or secondary education majors. They examined these competencies in order to ascertain the relationship between psychology and education, the history of education, major debates in contemporary education, and readings of the famous philosophers of education. They found no program that gave student teachers even an *introduction* to each of these four domains (126). The commonality, which they found in all but three programs, was for students to take a course focused on cultural diversity and multiculturalism. Important texts were written by Anita Woolfolk, Jonathan Kozol, Henry Giroux, Paulo Freire, and Gloria Ladson-Billings, who terms the teaching competencies desired as "culturally relevant teaching." Victimization issues were prominent. The authors found only one course syllabus in a single program that offered any readings presenting a countervailing view that there is universally valuable knowledge (129). In three-fourths of the courses devoted to issues in education policy, there was no indication that students were being taught about the major debates such as high-stakes tests, performance-based accountability, and vouchers (131). E. D. Hirsh's advocacy of a core knowledge program was found on only one recommended reading list and on one other syllabus. The authors state that, based on four syllabi, professors were even teaching students to distrust formal assessments and there was no evidence that teachers were being prepared to teach so as to maximize student performance on standardized tests (140). Only two schools used videotaping of student teaching and one school used audiotaping (140). It appears that colleges of education have uneven curriculum requirements for teachers. Even with specific concerns, there is a dearth of knowledge (viable research) linking teacher preparation program structures and content to outcomes such as the knowledge, skills, and dispositions of the graduating teachers or the achievement of students (Richardson and Roosevelt, 126). According to Richardson and Roosevelt, the evaluative frame of mind has not yet penetrated teacher education programs. Yet, in 2000, seventy-four percent of the states required written tests of basic skills for those teachers entering the occupation: fifty-eight percent had tests of content knowledge and forty-eight percent had written tests for subject-specific pedagogy (Education Week, 2000). Eighty-seven percent of test-takers passed Praxis II (Walsh, 2004, 234); further, all candidates from Teach for America passed the Principles of Learning for Teaching section, which is based on course-work to which Teach for America students have had no exposure! Critics also cite the success of instructors in the armed forces who teach well and with consequences without specialized teacher education. Based on the research of Steiner and what can be assumed from NASM requirements, the pedagogical content of the tests produced by ETS and that of the NBPTS are likely not closely related to teacher effectiveness.

There is surprising consensus on the importance of student teaching and mentorship programs although these major components of teacher education programs are today considered wanting and in need of major reforms. (Attachment to a believable idea can replace empirical data.) Confidence in student teaching may derive from an analogy with medical education but this analogy doesn't hold up. The aspiring doctor is anxious to put his newly acquired research knowledge into practice with live patients. The music student teacher is *not* equipped to approach student teaching with a repertoire of the latest research on developmentally appropriate and sequential student learning—the attitude is more one of "moving on" from college coursework to something completely new—often a passive observational experience until the prospective teacher sees how "it" is done.

PRESENT EVALUATION OF TEACHERS

Teachers are commonly evaluated by a rating scale, the primary method in use for nearly a hundred years. Charlotte Danielson (2002, 87) of ETS recommends that school administrators use a rating scale consisting of about fifteen "traits": knowledge of students, flexibility and responsiveness, contributing to the school and district, organizing physical space, managing student behavior, knowledge of content and pedagogy, selecting instructional goals, establishing a culture for learning, designing coherent instruction, growing and developing professionally, using questioning and discussion techniques, managing classroom procedures, engaging students in learning, maintaining accurate records, and communicating clearly and accurately.

One wonders why principals go to this trouble—the ratings are strictly pro forma, as fewer than one percent of teachers receive anything other than the highest marks on the summary evaluation report (Pajak and Arrington, 2004, 237, citing M. J. McGrath, "The Human Dynamics of Personnel Evaluation," *School Administrator,* 57(9) 1–8, p. 2).

The promise of the NBPTS is only marginally better. The process of setting NBPTS standards was driven largely by education associations that form the majority of its supporters and board (Rotherham and Mead, 2004, 33). The focus of NBPTS is on process, attitudes, and beliefs, rather than measurable knowledge and skills. With the focus on teacher behaviors rather than student achievement and little research on students' learning, one wonders about the justification for the resources that have been poured into developing and promoting NBPTS certification. States are not particularly helpful in clarifying the standards for teachers; the Arizona teacher standards say, "know major facts and assumptions that are central to the discipline (Walsh 2004, 247). Perhaps states should not regulate that which they cannot objectively measure—nor should NASM.

RECRUITING OF TEACHERS

NASM recommends preadmission tests for music education majors but few HS graduates who aspire to teach are likely to be turned away. A change has occurred in applicants to the teaching profession. In the 1960s, one in four new teachers scored in the top ten percent of their high school graduating classes. By 1992, this had dropped to one in ten (Boyd, et al. 2004, 152). Effective recruitment is critical as it is almost impossible to fail in the music education curriculum. — *But what is retention rate? (self-selection out of music teacher prep)*

SUMMARY

Palmer is correct that too much of our thinking has been rooted in theories of evaluation and learning that are nearly a century old. Steiner is also correct—use of a taxonomy is a way to begin. The recent taxonomies of Anderson (2001, a revision of the Bloom) and Marzano (2001) allow for serious consideration of the latest thinking in cognitive psychology. Delandshere (2002) encourages evaluators to think of assessment as inquiry, that knowledge is definable outside the individual and independent of context; suggesting, however, that we move from "to know" to "knowing." Knowing is knowledge in action, which suggests that if learning is controlled by the situation, then teaching consists of structuring the environment to produce the outcomes (1471). Elliott would find this argument for assessment compatible with his approach to a philosophy of music education. However, once music educators give careful consideration to the plethora of suggestions about assessment emanating from education, it is of primary importance that we give equal consideration to the many dimensions of teaching and learning where music *differs* from most, if not all, other disciplines. An unfortunate outcome of the opportunity presented by the reform movement would be that we accept, as valid, evaluation strategies from education that only "could" apply to outcomes in music; that is, we adopt strategies that are not specific to music. These strategies have been accepted because they satisfy advocates and those members of the profession too busy to become familiar with the enormous discipline of educational assessment. Our basic goals continue to be providing an opportunity for much of the population to gain a better understanding of music and to experience the excitement and fulfillment of participation. For meaningful change, our focus must be on the core of music, not on those fields touched by music. To initially develop assessment strategies that will aid teaching and learning, we might take John Goodlad's advice (2004, and Goodlad, Mantle-Bromley, and Goodlad, 2004) to consider renewal, not reform, and proceed by analyzing the musical and human qualities of today's best music educators and their proficient students and not take on all of the problems schooling is presently facing.

WORKS CITED

Anderson, L. 2003. *Classroom Assessment: Enhancing the Quality of Teacher Decision Making*. Mahway, NJ: Lawrence Erlbaum Associates, Publishers.

Anderson, L. and D. R. Krathwohl. 2001. *A Taxonomy for Learning, Teaching, and Assessing: A Revision of Bloom's Taxonomy of Educational Objectives*. New York: Longman.

Blakeslee, M. 2004. "Assembling the Arts Education Jigsaw." *Arts Education Policy Review*, 105(4), March/April: 31–36.

Boyd, D., H. Lankford., S. Loeb., and J. Wyckoff. 2004. "The Preparation and Recruitment of Teachers: A Labor-market Framework." In *A Qualified Teacher in Every Classroom: Appraising Old Answers and New Ideas*. F. M. Hess, A. J. Rotherham, and K. Walsh, eds. 149–71. Cambridge, MA: Harvard University Press.

Brophy, T. 2003. "Developing and Implementing Standards-based Assessments." In *Benchmarks in Action: A Guide to Standards-based Assessment in*

Music. C. A. Lindeman, ed. 1–16. Reston, VA: MENC: The National Association for Music Education.

Brown, C. 2000. "A Response to Anthony J. Palmer, 'Consciousness Studies and a Philosophy of Music Education,'" *Philosophy of Music Education Review*, Fall, 2.

Bruner, C. 2004. "Rethinking the Evaluation of Family Strengthening Strategies: Beyond Traditional Program Evaluation Models." *The Evaluation Exchange*, X (2), Summer: 24–25, 27.

Carr, J., and D. Harris. 2001. *Succeeding with Standards: Linking Curriculum, Assessment, and Action Planning*. Alexandria, VA: Association for Supervision and Curriculum Development

Cohen, D. K. (1995). "What Standards for National Standards?" *Phi Delta Kappan*, 76(10): 751–57.

Consortium of National Arts Education Associations. 1995. *Opportunity-to-learn Standards for Arts Education*. Reston, VA: Author.

Csikszentmihalyi, M., and B. Schneider. 2000. *Becoming Adult: How Teenagers Prepare for the World of Work*. New York: Basic Books.

Dance, Music, Theatre, Visual Arts: What Every Young American Should Know and Be Able to Do in the Arts: National Standards for Arts Education. 1994. Reston, VA: Music Educators National Conference.

Danielson, C. 2002. *Enhancing Student Achievement: A Framework for School Improvement*. Alexandria, VA: Association for Supervision and Curriculum Development.

Danielson, C., and T. McGreal. 2000. *Teacher Evaluation to Enhance Professional Practice*. Alexandria, VA: Association for Supervision and Curriculum Development.

Darling-Hammond, L. 2004. "Standards, Accountability, and School Reform." *Teachers College Record: Special Issue: Testing, Teaching and Learning*, 106(6), June: 1047–95.

Delandshere, G. 2002. "Assessment as Inquiry." *Teachers College Record*, 104 (7): 1461–84.

Duluth *New Tribune*. 2004. "State Social Studies, Science Standards Passed." Posted May 18.

Economist. 2004. "Few Are Chosen." 372(8382), July 3: 15.

Education Week. 2000. "Quality Counts: A Report on Education in the 50 States." Washington, DC: Author: 7.

Eisner, E. 2002. "The Kind of Schools We Need." *Phi Delta Kappan*, 83(8): 576–583.

Foulkes, A. E. 2004. "Weakened Immunity: How the Food and Drug Administration Caused Recent Vaccine-supply Problems." *The Independent Review*, IX (1) Summer: 31–54.

Gong, B., and E. W. Reidy. 1996. "Assessment and Accountability in Kentucky's School Reform." In *Performance-based Student Assessment: Challenges and Possibilities*. J. B Baron and D. P. Wolf, eds. 215–33.

Ninety-fifth Yearbook of the National Society for the Study of Education, Part I.

Goodlad, J. 2004. *Romances with Schools*. New York: McGraw Hill.

Goodlad, J., C. Mantle-Bromley., and S. J. Goodlad. 2004. *Education for Everyone*. San Francisco: Jossey-Bass.

Gordon, E. 1967. "A Three-year Longitudinal Predictive Validity Study of the Musical Aptitude Profile." *Studies in the Psychology of Music*, V, Iowa City: University of Iowa Press.

Ingram, D., K. Louis, and R. G. Schroeder. 2004. "Accountability Policies and Teacher Decision Making: Barriers to the Use of Data to Improve Practice." *Teachers College Record: Special Issue: Testing, Teaching and Learning*, 106(6), June: 1258–87.

Jorgensen, M. A. 2004. "And There Is Much Left to Do." In *Toward Coherence Between Classroom Assessment and Accountability*. M. Wilson, ed. 103rd Yearbook of the National Society for the Study of Education, Part II. Chicago: University of Chicago Press.

Lindeman, C. A. (ed.) 2003. *Benchmarks in Action: A Guide to Standards-based Assessment in Music*. Reston, VA: MENC: The National Association for Music Education, 31 and 41.

Linn, R. L. 2003. "Requirements for Measuring Adequate Yearly Progress." *Policy Brief 6*. Los Angeles: CRESST.

Linn, R. L, E. L. Baker., and D. W. Betebenner. 2002. "Accountability Systems: Implications of Requirements of the No Child Left Behind Act of 2001." *Educational Researcher*, 31(6): 3–16.

Magnuson, K. A., M. K. Meyers, C. J. Ruhm., and J. Waldfogel. 2004. "Inequality in Preschool Education and School Readiness." *American Educational Research Journal*, 41(1), Spring: 115–57.

Martella, J. 2004. "The Road from Research to Outcomes." *The Evaluation Exchange*, X (2), Summer: 13.

Marzano, R. J. 2001. *Designing a New Taxonomy of Education Objectives*. Thousand Oaks, CA: Corwin Press.

Meier, D. 2000. *Will Standards Save Public Education?* Boston: Beacon Press, 20.

——— D. 2004. "No Politician Left Behind." *The Nation*, June 14, 6–8.

Music Educators National Conference. 1996. Paul Lehman (chair). *Performance Standards for Music: Strategies and Benchmarks for Assessing Progress Toward the National Standards, Grades PreK–12*. Reston, VA: MENC.

NAMM. 2003. Retrieved June 23, 2004, from http://www.namm.com/pressroom/pressreleases/2003_April 21.html.

NASM. Handbook 2003–2004: *Standards and Guidelines for Institutions and Majors*. (2003). Reston, VA: Author.

No Child Left Behind Act of 2001. 2002. Pub L. No. 107-110, 115 Stat. 1425.

Olson, D. R. 2003. *Psychological Theory and Educational Reform:How School Remakes Mind and Society*. Cambridge, UK: Cambridge University Press.

Pajak, E., and A. Arrington. 2004. "Empowering a Profession: Rethinking the Roles of Administrative Evaluation and Instructional Supervision in Improving Teacher Quality." In *Developing the Teacher Workforce.* M.A. Smylie and D. Miretzky, eds. 103rd yearbook of the National Society for the Study of Education, Part I. Chicago: University of Chicago Press.

Palmer, A. J. 2000. "Consciousness Studies and a Philosophy of Music Education." *Philosophy of Music Education Review,* 8(2) Fall: 99–110.

Popkewitz, T. 2004 "The Alchemy of the Mathematics Curriculum: Inscriptions and the Fabrication of the Child." *American Education Research Journal,* Spring 2004, 41(1): 3–34.

Reimer, B. 2003. *A Philosophy of Music Education: Advancing the Vision,* 3rd edition, Upper Saddle River, NJ: Prentice Hall.

Richardson, V., and Roosevelt, D. 2004. "Teacher Preparation and the Improvement of Teacher Education." In *Developing the Teacher Workforce.* M. A. Smylie and D. Miretsky, eds. 103rd Yearbook of the National Society for the Study of Education, Part I. Chicago: University of Chicago Press, 11–47.

Rotherham, A. J., and S. Mead. 2004. "Back to the Future: The History and Politics of State Teacher Licensure and Certification." In *A Qualified Teacher in Every Classroom: Appraising Old Answers and New Ideas.* F. M. Hess, A. J. Rotherham, and K. Walsh, eds. Cambridge, MA: Harvard University Press.

Sabol, R. F. 2004. "The Assessment Context: Part Two." *Arts Education Policy Review,* 105(4), March/April: 3–7.

Scruton, R. 1997. *The Aesthetics of Music.* New York: Oxford University Press.

Shonkoff, J. 2004. "Evaluating Early Childhood Services: What's Really Behind the Curtain." *The Evaluation Exchange,* X (2), Summer: 3–4.

Smith, P. 2004. "Curricular Transformation: Why We Need It: How to Support It." *Change,* 36(1) January/February: 28–35.

Smithson, J. L. 2004. "Converging Paths: Common Themes in Making Assessments Useful to Teachers and System." *Towards Coherence Between Classroom Assessment and Accountability,* 103rd Yearbook of the National Society for the Study of Education, Part II. Wilson, Mark (Ed.), Chicago: University of Chicago Press.

Steiner, D. with S. D. Rozen. 2004. "Preparing Tomorrow's Teachers: An Analysis of Syllabi from a Sample of America's Schools of Education." In *Appraising Old Answers and New Ideas.* F. M. Hess., A. J. Rotherham., and K. Walsh, eds. 119–48. Cambridge, MA: Harvard University Press.

Strike, K. A. 2004. "Community, the Missing Element of School Reform: Why Schools Should Be More like Congregations Than Banks." *American Journal of Education,* 110(3) May: 215–232.

Walsh, K. 2004. "A Candidate-Centered Model for Teacher Preparation and Licensure." In *Appraising Old Answers and New Ideas*. F. M. Hess., A. J. Rotherham, and K. Walsh, eds. 223–53. Cambridge, MA: Harvard University Press.

Xue, Y., and S. J. Meisels. 2004. "Early Literacy Instruction and Learning in Kindergarten: Evidence from the Early Childhood Longitudinal Study—Kindergarten Class of 1998–1999." *American Educational Research Journal*, 41(1): 191–229, Spring.

Part III

Theatre Education

Chapter 5

Assessment Through Drama

Robert J. Landy

ASSUMPTIONS, ASSESSMENTS, AND EVALUATIONS

Whether creators or consumers of art, we tend to approach an art experience with a set of assumptions. Assumptions are preconceived notions concerning some specific content based upon one's personal beliefs and value system, rather than empirical evidence. Some artists believe that the purpose of art-making is to illuminate, reflect, or enhance everyday life. Others think that art-making serves a narcissistic need on the part of the artist, or serves a utilitarian, decorative purpose, or even a spiritual purpose, akin to worship. Consumers and critics also have a variety of explanations of why they attend art events. For some, the event offers a reflection of reality, one that stimulates feeling and thought. For others, the event offers an enjoyable escape from reality. Still others go to concerts or plays or art exhibits for social reasons.

These assumptions carried by art-makers and consumers might be seen as morally based: for example, "Art reveals the struggle between the forces of good and evil," or "It is good for you to play an instrument or to go to the theatre." They might be seen as intellectually based: for instance, "In order to write a story, I must have a deep understanding of my characters in their milieu," or "When I attend an art opening, I am able to see the world in a new way." Or assumptions about art can be conceptualized in many other ways, including spiritually, politically, and emotionally.

For some nonartists and nonconsumers of art, the art experience is a frill or worse, an affectation, that serves no useful purpose in society. When these individuals are in powerful positions, responsible for allocating funds and resources to various educational and health enterprises, they threaten the very existence of the art experience within institutions. To complicate matters, these same people might well support the existence of museums and libraries and concert halls and theatres, assuming that they are economically and culturally significant indicators of civilization. But when it comes to thinking about the creation of new art beyond the institutions, their assumptions might radically change. They might not even think of the exhibits in a museum or a library as art. Artifacts are often safer and less threatening than art that is a living, evolving organism that often serves no discernible utilitarian purpose.

In a culture that values science above art, that values product over process, that values the real over the fictional, stereotype over prototype, surface over depth, function over form, matter over mind, quantity over quality—where does that leave the artist and her audience? And where does that leave arts educators and arts therapists who assume that the making and viewing of art have transformative qualities for students and clients?

Before we can speak about ways to assess through art, we need to be aware of the assumptions of all those involved in the art-making, consuming, and administrating process. This writer, who has played all those roles, begins with a central assumption—that the processes of teaching and learning, of developing intellectually, psychologically, spiritually, and socially throughout the life span, can be significantly enhanced through engaging in the arts.

Assessment is a form of interview or test that generally precedes some task in order to judge an individual or group's level of functioning and/or readiness to perform that task. A young person can be given several art media and assessed as to which one is the best match. Various art media are used to assess psychological levels of functioning of individuals. Examples include: Kinetic Family Drawing (Elin and Nucho, 1979) and House-Tree-Person (Buck, 1966) in art therapy; and Role Profiles (Landy, et al. 2003) and the Diagnostic Role-Playing Test (Johnson, 1988) in drama therapy.

In arts education, assessment can be useful not only at the start of a process, but also in midstream. In a grade five drama class, for example, a teacher who has been working improvisationally might wonder if it is time to begin work on text. To assess her students' readiness to work with text, she might ask them to read a scene from a play and follow up with questions to test their reading and interpretive skills. Generally speaking, however, when a test is applied in the midst of an ongoing learning process, it is called a formative evaluation rather than an assessment.

Evaluation is a test, interview, or portfolio review that follows the completion of a task in order to determine how well an individual or group has mastered that task. Evaluators attempt to measure both the quantity and quality of mastery. Mastery includes, but is not limited to, demonstrated forms of cognitive learning and affective and psychomotor development. In evaluating drama, the evaluator often applies a set of criteria to determine how well a student has acted a role, performed an improvisational scene, or critiqued a play. As mentioned above, evaluation can also be formative when applied to an ongoing learning process. For example, a group of students might be learning ways to use their imagination through theatre games. Having assessed their readiness to begin, the teacher engages them in a ten-week experience. After five weeks, she presents a series of theatre games to determine how well the group has mastered the fundamentals of imaginative thought and action.

Assumptions are based on thoughts, feelings, and values that are not necessarily conscious. Assumptions tend to be rather subjective, even though groups of like-minded people within a common community or culture often share similar assumptions about the nature of reality, and even fantasy. Assessments and evaluations are supposedly more objective, based on specified criteria pertaining usually to some theoretical model, whether implicit or explicit.

WHY ASSESS THROUGH DRAMA?

As a drama educator, I may assume that for all ninth graders, both acting in a play and viewing professional actors perform a play are equally positive learning experiences. However, if I assess a specific group of ninth graders, I might discover that not all are ready to either perform or to view plays. There might be psychological and physiological reasons why some are not ready to participate in both dramatic experiences. Had I not assessed the group, but rather evaluated them after they performed in a play and viewed a professional production, I might have discovered that one part of the experience was meaningless or even harmful to one or more students. Understanding the differences between assessment and evaluation would have been helpful in this case for the teacher to better understand the nature and needs of her students.

Generally speaking, one assesses through drama for two reasons: to determine the readiness of a person to perform or witness a certain dramatic task; and to determine one's dramatic competency based upon specific criteria. When assessment is given in the midst of an ongoing process, its purposes are the same.

In relationship to dramatic activities, whether educational or therapeutic, dramatic forms of assessment are preferable to more generic ones that measure cognitive or psychological competencies. For example, it would be preferable to measure one's ability to play roles through a role-playing form of assessment (see, for example, Johnson, 1988, Landy, et al., 2003). As with any other form of assessment, researchers, educators, and therapists look for those that are most valid, that is, that measure what they intend to measure. As it is absurd to measure the area of a room with a barometer, it is equally inappropriate to measure someone's ability to play roles with the Wechsler Intelligence Scale.

We assess through drama, then, to determine both readiness to engage in drama and dramatic competencies. But what if a researcher or practitioner would want to apply dramatic assessment to individuals engaged in nondramatic activities? Is there a connection between what an actor does on stage and what a human being does in everyday life? Would such a link risk straining the validity of a dramatic assessment instrument?

The *theatricum mundi* metaphor of the world as a stage and people as actors has been around for millennia. It has been used so often in the English language that it has become a cliché. The relationship between everyday life and drama cannot be empirically verified. And yet philosophers, poets, and social scientists have long argued, some quite persuasively (see, for example, Cooley, 1922; Goffman, 1959; Burke, 1972; Brissett and Edgley, 1975; Wilshire, 1982) that the metaphor reveals a rich and complex understanding of human behavior. If we accept their collective wisdom, we may be able to justify a dramatic assessment of behavior in everyday life. If so, then we can view dramatic assessment as a way of measuring someone's mastery of and readiness to take on and play out roles in everyday life.

The persistence of the dramatic metaphor in analyzing individual behavior and social life lends further credence to the potential for the applications of dramatic assessments and evaluations to various facets of social life, most notably, education and therapy.

WHEN TO ASSESS/EVALUATE THROUGH DRAMA

As mentioned above, assessments are generally given at the beginning of a process. Evaluation can be given in the midst of a process to help individuals find better ways to engage in the ongoing process, or at the conclusion of a process to determine the depth and breadth of learning. In that assessment and evaluation often get mixed up in reference to arts education, it is important to be mindful of the differences. The contemporary emphasis on tests that sum up a student's learning also impacts on arts education. Teachers who understand the value of assessment and formative evaluation are often pushed into relying solely on summative evaluations.

As an example, the New York State Department of Education (1996) has developed standards for students in theatre that include:

1. Creating, performing and participating in theatre
2. Knowing and using theatre materials and resources
3. Responding to and analyzing works of dramatic art
4. Understanding the cultural dimensions and contributions of the dramatic arts

Each standard is broken down into specific performance criteria at the elementary, intermediate, and commencement (secondary) levels. All students are evaluated following a course of study as to how well they have realized these performance criteria. If these standards were to require assessments and formative evaluations, the teacher might glean new information to guide her student's ongoing learning process.

Optimally, it is best to assess at the beginning of a learning/ therapeutic process. It is best to apply formative evaluation in the middle. And it is best to apply summative evaluation at the end. When all forms of measurement are applied, the teacher has many ways to guide the learning process and to help students achieve mastery.

WHO SHOULD ASSESS/EVALUATE?
WHO SHOULD BE ASSESSED/EVALUATED?

If it is true that teachers play multiple roles in the classroom, one role that all teachers play is that of evaluator. It would be hard to imagine a teacher not playing this role. Are teachers also assessors or do others determine levels of readiness and mastery before the teacher begins her lessons? In classes where students are ability-ranked, administrators have been responsible for the assessments. In some cases, school psychologists and/or social workers contribute to the assessments and determinations as to student placements. In other cases, students themselves make the determination as to whether they are prepared and interested in taking, for example, a drama class.

Formative and summative evaluations are generally the domain of teachers or of standardized tests administered by teachers or trained personnel. Peer reviews in a drama class are also highly useful, serving the purposes of formative and summative evaluation. Further, some teachers will encourage self-evaluations, where students develop means to determine their development in, for example, interpreting a character or writing a scene. When taken together, all three approaches to assessment and evaluation—by teachers and school staff, by peers and by self-reflection, present a full picture of the possibilities.

As to who should be assessed, it seems clear that anyone willing to engage in drama should be assessed. This would include all school-based students, special needs students, in fact all individuals throughout the life span, from very young to very old. This would also include individuals in a wide range of community-based and institutional settings from preschools to hospitals, clinics, religious centers, museums, prisons, and so on. All human beings learn dramatically in the most natural of ways, without any prior instruction. When dramatic learning is applied by educators and therapists, then they are responsible for assessing an individual's readiness to engage in given dramatic tasks.

WHAT SHOULD BE ASSESSED/ EVALUATED TIIROUGH DRAMA?

One issue of assessment concerns how teachers or administrators determine a student's readiness to study drama. What skills should the student possess before beginning formal study? It has been argued (see Courtney, 1974; Jennings, 1997; Landy, 1975, 1993, 1996) that drama is an inborn primary process of learning, and that the earliest forms of human expression through sensory-motor means are dramatic in nature. If this is true, then it could be that all individuals, having learned about their bodies in relationship to the natural and social worlds, are inherently dramatic learners. As such, any assessment of readiness should concern their particular strengths and weaknesses in dramatizing, rather than a determination of whether or not they can dramatize. Having said this, the next question becomes: what kinds of strengths and weaknesses should be measured?

In response to this question, we need to take a theoretical turn to understand the basic dimensions of the dramatic experience. I have written elsewhere (see Landy, 1993, 2000, 2001) that the two most primary dimensions of all dramatic activity are the ability to take on and play out roles, and the ability to tell or enact stories in role. While engaged in drama, whether in play, role-play, improvisational activity, ritual, or theatrical production, one takes on a role that is different from oneself and while in role, tells or performs a story. Given this point of view, an assessment would determine an individual's ability to take on and play out one or more roles, and an individual's ability to tell a story or stories while in role. Stories can be enacted through words, sound, and movement, or some combination. Given a set of age-based standards referenced to role-taking and story-making, a student would be measured on her ability to do both according to the standards.

Throughout the course of a dramatic process, students can also be given formative and summative evaluations to determine whether they have taken on and played out roles effectively and whether they have told or enacted stories effectively. These dimensions could be further specified so that the evaluator looks at the quantity of roles taken as well as the quality of roles enacted. In a like manner, both the form and content of the storymaking and performing can be evaluated.

Referring to the New York State theatre standards, it becomes clear that other dimensions are also to be measured. These include knowledge of resources and materials, criticism of theatrical performances, and historical and cultural understandings. Again, one's choice of standards and criteria will guide one's decision on what aspects of the dramatic experience are significant to assess and evaluate. Having said this, it is important for educators to consider significance. Here, too, they would need to turn to theoretical considerations. If they feel that the most significant aspect of the dramatic experience concerns role and story, then their criteria would be based on those considerations. If, however, they are mandated by the state to view the dramatic experience in terms of criteria set by given standards, then they would need to reconcile their approach with that of the required curriculum. In the example of New York State standards, that would not be too hard to do as Standard 1, engagement in creation and performance of theatre, incorporates both role and story.

HISTORICAL OVERVIEW

The formal discipline of Educational Drama and Theatre (variously called Creative Drama, Dramatic Education, Educational Theatre, Drama-in-Education, Theatre-in-Education, and Developmental Drama, among others) has been around in the English-speaking world since the early twentieth century. The field developed primarily in England and America. Although each country has its own sources, cultural influences, and pioneers, practitioners on both sides of the Atlantic developed their work initially along a similar trajectory. The early work of the British English teacher, Henry Caldwell Cook (1917), pointed to the primacy of play as a central method of learning. Cook was instrumental in teaching literary texts to children through a form of dramatic enactment. Cook provided an early philosophy and methodology of dramatic education. Sounding very much like his American contemporary, John Dewey, Cook (1917) wrote: "Proficiency and learning come not from reading and listening but from action; from doing and from experience."

Around the same time, influenced by Dewey (1966) and the eighteenth-century progressive educational philosopher, Heinrich Pestalozzi (1951), a number of American educators began to experiment with dramatic approaches to classroom learning. The most influential was Winifred Ward from Evanston, Illinois. Like Cook,

Ward (1930) taught children language arts through improvisational drama. Her approach, which came to be known as creative dramatics, was widely emulated through the twentieth century in elementary and middle school throughout the United States.

The American tradition tended to be driven by practice. Oftentimes the process of learning subject matter through drama was subjugated to the product of performing a school play, a tradition that still pervades American drama education.

The British tradition also had a strong practical thrust exemplified in the work of Peter Slade and Brian Way, among many others. Complementing the drama work, a tradition of movement education also developed, inspired by the work of Rudolf Laban (1960), and leading to a confluence of movement and drama that later coalesced in a training course at the Sesame Institute in London. However, British drama educators also began to ask more philosophical and psychological questions, pertaining to the effects of dramatic processes on human learning. Thus we find Peter Slade (1954) and Richard Courtney (1973) attempting, in separate publications, to lay out a developmental sequence of learning through drama, both influence by Piaget's (1962) model of cognitive development. Following from this work Dorothy Heathcote (Johnson and O'Neill, 1991) and Gavin Bolton (1984) developed more constructivist theories and approaches, moving the work from prescriptive and developmental actions into a process of open-ended and challenging questions that led to and reflected upon the actions. When working with Heathcote and Bolton, children learned that drama was not only about physical action, but also about moments of contemplation and reflection and dialectical discussion.

Up to the 1980s in the United Kingdom, there was little attention paid to formal assessment and evaluation. The assumption held by many drama educators was that all children could and should engage in drama in schools and that by doing so, they would enhance their cognitive and imaginative capacities.

The American tradition diverged from that of the British in the 1960s. At that time, two separate approaches came into being. One was most influenced by the human potential movement of the 1960s, expressed in antiwar protests and the burgeoning liberation movements within oppressed and underrepresented communities. These activities were further informed by ideas articulated by psychologists such as Abraham Maslow (1963) and Carl Rogers (1961), philosophers such as Herbert Marcuse (1972) and Michael Polanyi

(1966), and such therapists and critics as Fritz Perls (1969) and Herbert Kohl (1970). A number of radical theatre groups, such as The Living Theatre, The Open Theatre, and El Teatro Campesino, also espoused this most liberal, if not radical approach to education. Around the same time, the Theatre-in-Education (TIE) movement began in England. This approach concerned building performances with individuals in a community around significant social issues. Like the more radical theatre companies, the TIE groups assumed that theatre serves a political and social function. Their politics tended to be radical and their social aims tended to be transformative.

The central assumption of many drama educators under these influences was that dramatic learning was transformative for both teacher and student. Standardized criteria and attention to set curricula were abandoned in favor of a subjective, phenomenological process driven by engagement in the here and now, rather than upon a completion of a final product.

The second trend concerned a more objective and precise approach to education. This approach can be best represented by the work of the educational psychologist Benjamin Bloom (1956), who attempted to quantify the learning experience in terms of observable behavioral objectives. Bloom and his colleagues specified three learning domains: cognition, affect, and psychomotor, identifying specific aspects of each in terms of quantifiable behaviors.

Bloom's influence in educational drama was first translated into practice when Ann Shaw (1970) created a taxonomy of behavioral objectives in creative drama. With this work and that of others who were reacting against the influence of the human potential movement on school curricula, drama teachers, like their peers working across the curriculum, began to consider the significance of stating specific aims and objectives of dramatic education and seeking out frameworks within which to measure students' ability to realize these aims. Shaw's work, although centered in dramatic experience, was very much couched within an educational psychological model of cognition and affect.

Another early framework, a more direct precursor of current school standards, was created in California in 1971. The framework, called *Drama/Theatre Framework for California Public Schools, a Process-Concept Framework for a Program in the Theatre Arts for All Students Kindergarten through Twelfth Grade* (Manley, et. al, 1971), aimed "to establish guidelines for theatre arts education as part of the general education of California school children." John Manley and his panel of theatre arts experts proceeded with their task with the precision of Shaw. Unlike Shaw, however, they did not view educational psychology as source material. And unlike Shaw, they did not specify behavioral objectives. Instead, they based their learning objectives fully in the art form, looking at theatre processes, activities, concepts, resources, and aims. As they defined their terms, the panel set the stage for later state standards in the theatre arts. For example, they define theatre processes as "the ways in which the student experiences the art: Originating, Performing, Producing and Responding." These specific processes later appear in twenty-first-century state standards.

Both the educational psychological approach of the taxonomy and the theatrical approach of the framework place the field of educational drama in a positivist philosophical position, ready and willing to be absorbed into the standards movement of twenty-first-century American education. Foreshadowing this trend, the British drama educator, David Hornbrook (1998), challenged theorists and practitioners internationally to further quantify their work and be held accountable for student achievement in drama and theatre.

In the early part of the twenty-first century, several states have developed standards in the visual and performing arts, pertaining to grades K–12. Many of the standards are similar to those of New York State, with some modification. For example, California, moving beyond its earlier framework, lists the following five: artistic perception; creative expression; historical and cultural context; aesthetic valuing; and connections, relations, and applications. With each attempt to specify the significant content to be learned in drama/theatre, the drafters of these standards act within the more conservative tradition, attempting to measure aesthetic learning through evaluating students' mastery of a given set of criteria. In applying these standards, educators are asked to engage primarily in summative evaluations rather than assessments or formative evaluations.

A related field developed alongside that of educational drama. By the late 1960s, several professionals in educational drama were also experimenting with therapeutic applications of drama and theatre processes. Their work, combined with others in the related fields of psychodrama and alternative theatre would come to be known as drama therapy. Drama therapy began as educational drama methods were extended to nonschool populations of physically disabled and emotionally disturbed individuals as well as those living in nontraditional settings, such as prisons and nursing

homes. Like their colleagues in educational drama, drama therapists sought to develop a new discipline in terms of objectives, treatment strategies, and outcomes. However, liberated from the con-
fines of public school systems, drama therapists looked to
psychological models for ways and means to conceptualize their
approaches to dramatic development.

Some in the field of drama therapy have directly taken on the
issue of assessment as it is an important aspect of clinical treatment.
In clinical terms, assessment is akin to diagnosis, the starting point
of most psychologically based clinical treatment. Psychological
assessment traditionally begins with the *Diagnostic and Statistical
Manual* (*DSM*), presently in its fourth edition. The manual is organized into sixteen diagnostic classes and also five axes with information to guide the clinician in making treatment and outcome decisions. The fifth axis, Global Assessment of Functioning, provides a
numerical score from 0 to 100, representing a range from very low
to superior functioning in a wide range of activities. Drama therapists as well as other creative arts therapists have developed their
own assessment instruments as a complement, supplement, or sub-
stitution for the *DSM*. Several examples follow.

ASSESSMENT THROUGH
DRAMA THERAPY

A number of assessment instruments have developed that focus on
the primacy of either story or role. The Dutch/British drama therapist, Alida Gersie (1991, 1997), developed a six-part story structure to assess a subject's ability to tell and dramatize stories. Gersie
asks her subjects to either tell or enact a story based on the following elements: landscape, character, dwelling place, obstacle, help-
mate, and resolution. Following the storymaking, Gersie assesses
the subject's storymaking abilities and determines how to best proceed
with treatment.

The Israeli-based drama therapist, Mooli Lahad, who trained with
Gersie, further specifies the storymaking approach. Lahad's (1992)
assessment instrument, Six-piece Story-making (6-PSM), intends to
measure the coping styles of people facing stress and trauma. Subjects are asked to draw pictures on a paper divided into six parts,
each part representing one of the following: a main character and
his/her place of residence; the mission or task of the character; a person or thing that will help the character fulfill his/her mission; the

obstacle that stands in the character's way; the way the character copes with the obstacle; the ending or continuation of the story.

After the artwork, subjects are asked to tell their stories. The stories are then analyzed by the drama therapist who applies a set of criteria regarding six basic coping styles. These styles are derived from Lahad's theoretical model, BASIC Ph., conceptualized as follows:

B, coping through Beliefs and values
A, coping through Affective means
S, coping through Social relationships
I, coping through Imaginative means
C, coping through Cognitive means
Ph, coping through Physical means

Information gleaned from 6-PSM enables the therapist to specify the subject's coping style, which may be located in one or more of the categories.

A third story-based assessment, Tell-A-Story (TAS), is one I developed (2001). The assessment begins with the following directions:

> I would like you to tell me a story. The story can be based upon something that happened to you or to somebody else in real life or it can be completely made up. The story must have at least one character.

The story can be told in a traditional verbal fashion or, for less verbal subjects, the story can be enacted through movement or through projective means, such as puppets. Following the storytelling, the assessor asks the subject to identify the character or characters in the story. For each character (not more than three), the assessor asks the subject to specify qualities and functions, aspects of my role theory (1993). The assessor also asks questions concerning the level of reality/fantasy, an understanding of the theme of the story, and the connection between the fiction of the story and the everyday life of the storyteller.

Through TAS, the assessor looks for ways to characterize the subject in terms of his ability to tell a story, to understand how the characters function within the story and how they relate to the storyteller's everyday life.

Two assessment instruments have been developed that focus primarily on role. The first, the Diagnostic Role-Playing Test (DRPT), was created by Johnson (1988), who created two versions of the test.

The first, DRPT 1, proceeds as the subject is asked to enact five roles—grandparent, bum, politician, teacher, lover. In the second, DRPT 2, the subject is provided the following directions:

> I am now going to ask you to do three scenes. After each one I will ask you some questions. Enact a scene between three beings in any way that you wish. Who or what these three beings are is up to you. Tell me when you are finished.

At the conclusion of each scene, the assessor poses the following questions: "Tell me in as much detail as you can what happened in that scene ... Now, describe the three beings, one at a time" (Johnson, 1988).

Unlike Lahad, Johnson is not looking to discern a particular coping style. But yet, like Lahad, he specifies a set of criteria through which he interprets the behavior of the subjects in role. His criteria are as follows:

1. Spontaneity
2. Ability to transcend reality
3. Role repertoire
4. Organization of scenes
5. Patterns in the dramatic content of scenes
6. Attitude toward enactment
7. Style of role-playing

Johnson's assessments have been used for research and treatment purposes with a range of subjects and clients, including schizophrenic adults and war veterans suffering from posttraumatic stress syndrome (see Johnson and Quinlan, 1993; James and Johnson, 1997). As with other drama therapy assessments, Johnson aims to measure the readiness of clients to engage in therapy as well as their present levels of functioning.

The second role-based assessment, Role Profiles, was one I developed (2001b, 2003) as an extension of my work in role theory (Landy, 1993, 2000). Role Profiles is a card sort that attempts to specify an individual's ability to see himself in terms of a series of seventy roles. The assessment proceeds according to the following instructions:

> This experience is intended to explore your personality as if it were made-up characters commonly found in plays, movies, and stories. You

will be given a stack of cards. On each card is the name of a *role*, which is a type of character you have probably seen in movies and plays or read about in stories. Please shuffle the cards thoroughly. Place each card in one of four groups that best describes how you feel about yourself right now. Each group is labeled by a large card which says: *I Am This, I Am Not This, I Am Not Sure If I Am This*, and *I Want To Be This*. Try to group the cards as quickly as possible. Any questions? When you are ready, begin. Be sure to place each card in one group only.

Following the card sort into the four categories, the assessor asks the subject a number of questions, looking for ways to measure the quantity and quality of roles generated by the subject. Criteria applied in Role Profiles again refer back to my role theory. Consistent with role theory, the assessor is looking to see whether the subject is able to view himself in a balanced way. Balance would imply a relatively equal distribution of roles between "I Am This" and "I Am Not This," and a lesser quantity of cards in the grouping "I Want To Be This." If there are few entries in "I'm Not Sure If I Am This," the subject would be relatively clear as to his identity. If this category becomes large, this may be an indication of immaturity or uncertainty or role confusion.

There are certain basic guidelines the assessor follows in documenting the results of the role profile. The guidelines are written in the form of questions. The following are examples:

1. How does the subject respond to the directions? Does he ask for more clarity? Does he jump right into the process? Does he manifest any anxiety or resistance to the process?
2. How does the subject sort the cards? How does he decide upon the grouping? Does he sort quickly or slowly, deliberately or impulsively? Does he engage with the assessor during the card sort? How does he use time and organize space?
3. Which roles has the subject placed in each group? How many are in each group? Are the groups balanced or unbalanced?
4. Are there any charged roles, that is, roles that seem to be troubling or confusing or evocative of some emotional response? What are they? Where does the subject eventually place these roles? How does the subject react to these roles?
5. Which roles seem most and least important? Why?
6. What is the connection among roles within a single group? Are there contradictory roles within a single group, that is, mother and father within the group "I Am This"?

7. What is the connection among roles within different groups, that is, in the child in "I Am This" and the adult in "I'm Not Sure If I Am This"?
8. Is the subject able to discern patterns, that is, a view of the connected roles he plays in his family, or does he see the roles as disconnected and fragmentary?
9. Is the subject able to recognize his own identity within the roles and groupings or does he see the results as arbitrary and meaningless?
10. Is the subject able to discern certain contradictions among the roles, that is, hero and average person, and accept that two or many contradictory roles can be part of his role profile? Or does the subject tend to dismiss contradiction and attempt to view himself in a singular way, that is, the visionary hero-artist on a spiritual quest?
11. How does the subject dismantle the groupings and reshuffle the deck? Is there a willingness to close the process or to delay the closure? What kinds of feelings are expressed? Is the client in a balanced or unbalanced state? Does he express what he will do with the results of the test?

Taken together, these several approaches to assessment in drama therapy all point to the primacy of role and story in the dramatic experience and attempt to measure only the present functioning of an individual. The information gleaned from the assessments is also used to determine the individual's readiness for treatment.

APPLYING DRAMA THERAPY ASSESSMENTS TO EDUCATIONAL DRAMA AND THEATRE

Generally speaking, drama therapy is not practiced in schools. And yet, there may be ways that the various therapeutically based assessments could be modified to help drama/theatre teachers to both think about assessment and actually assess students. In that all the drama therapy assessments concern role and story, the teacher might consider these aspects of the dramatic experience as primary. If so, then at the beginning of a learning process she might want to assess the readiness of her students to take on and play out roles and to tell stories through language, sound, and/or movement.

To assess storytelling and storymaking competencies, the teacher could apply a modified version of either 6-PSM or TAS. Both instruments could be used throughout the grades, leaning more heavily upon the visual 6-PSM for the younger grades. Gersie's structure of landscape, character, dwelling place, obstacle, help-mate, and resolution could also be applied at various grade levels.

In using Lahad's 6-PSM, should the teacher apply the criteria specified in the model of BASIC Ph in order to assess her students? In that we are discussing a pedagogical rather than a psychological approach, it would seem that the teacher would look to other criteria for measurement purposes. Again, the instrument would be used to determine readiness for further work in storytelling and storymaking. Criteria then would concern responses to questions such as the following:

1. Is the student able to sketch her story through the given six-part structure?
2. Is there a progression from character to mission to helper to obstacle to means of coping to resolution?
3. Is the student able to tell a story based on her artwork?
4. If the student can tell the story, is she ready to dramatize the story?

In answering these and related questions, the teacher may be able to assess the readiness of students to engage in more advanced dramatic activities, such as story dramatization. Further, she may be able to make more qualitative judgments as to the depth of the storymaking and storytelling process.

Likewise, teachers can make use of my *Tell-A-Story*. Although the criteria for assessment are based in my role theory and meant to be oriented toward therapeutic issues, several could be easily adapted to educational concerns. For example, the teacher could ask students to speak about the qualities and functions of the characters in their stories. The kind of questions the teacher asks would be similar to those I specified (2001). Examples in terms of descriptive qualities of characters are:

1. How do the characters look (physical/somatic qualities)?
2. How smart are the characters (cognitive qualities)?
3. How do the characters feel?
4. What are the characters' beliefs and values (affective qualities)?
5. How social, spiritual, and creative are the characters (social, spiritual, aesthetic qualities)?

Examples in terms of function include: In the story, what does each character want most of all? How do each character's choices affect other characters in the story? Such questions can help the teacher assess a student's understanding of character and motivation.

Further, questions about the theme of the story and the style of presentation, whether reality or fantasy-based, can provide the teacher information about the student's understanding of narrative and dramatic structure and form. These higher-level skills are most appropriate to secondary-level students, but even a simple descriptive understanding of a character as a physical, emotional, and social being can be given by elementary school children. This information can be useful to a teacher needing to assess her students' readiness to work in role.

To assess role-taking and role-playing readiness and competency, the teacher can apply Johnson's DRPT 1. The teacher can ask children throughout the elementary grades to enact the five roles specified by Johnson: grandparent, bum, politician, teacher, and lover. If this instrument were repeated at selected grades, for instance, grades four, eight, and twelve, it might be efficacious to compare the responses. As specified by Johnson, subjects are videotaped when engaging in the role-play. If this method is repeated in a school setting, the videotapes made at different times could be gleaned for comparative data as to mastery of the roles.

In the secondary grades, a teacher could apply Johnson's DRPT 2, asking students to enact three beings. In determining the results of both measures, teachers could apply some or all of Johnson's seven criteria. For example, in assessing the role-play of a fourth grader, the teacher might look at the student's abilities to act spontaneously, to transcend reality, and to organize scenes. In assessing a tenth grader, additional criteria could be examined, including: role repertoire, organization of scenes, patterns in the dramatic content of scenes, attitude toward enactment, and style of role-playing.

My Role Profiles might also be applied to a classroom context, with some age-based modification of role types. In fact, students could be asked to develop their own taxonomy of roles based on types of characters familiar to them in stories, movies, television, video, and plays. Rather than sorting a given set of cards, students could be asked to create their own and place them in categories similar to those I specified. The teachers would assess the students' abilities to understand the concept of role and to give names to roles. Having established a baseline understanding of roles, the teacher and students might choose to move into work on character studies and/or the writing of monologues and dialogues.

The thoughtful drama teacher/researcher would undoubtedly find other ways to apply these assessments to the drama classroom. In doing so, she would demonstrate a willingness to assess her students' competency and readiness to engage in a specified level of role-play and storymaking.

FUTURE DIRECTIONS

Shortly after the 9/11 terrorist attacks on the World Trade Center, *The New York Times* granted funds to several New York City–based educational theatre organizations for the purpose of working with children most deeply affected. One organization that was chosen, City Lights Youth Theatre, invited a drama therapist to create a model program, reasoning that with the dual perspectives of theatre and therapy, such a program would best suit the aesthetic and psychological needs of the children. The model created, "Standing Tall," was implemented with a group of fourth and fifth graders, all of whom had witnessed the attack on the twin towers outside their classroom window on the fourth day of school in 2001.

The central idea of the model was to enable the children to express their experience through taking on roles and telling and dramatizing stories. The role-taking and story dramatization would occur within a fictional community called "Standing Tall." The roles taken would be archetypal, pertaining to the dramatic nature of the actual attack and its aftermath. The three generic role types chosen by the drama therapist and children were hero, villain, and victim.

Following some fifteen hours of workshop, the drama therapist wrote a play based on the roles taken and stories told by the children. The children rehearsed and performed the play for the school community at the end of the semester.

A unique feature of this process was that the drama therapist worked directly with a teaching artist from City Lights and collaborated throughout with the educational theatre organization in preparing and implementing this experience. Further, both the drama therapist and teaching artist engaged fully with the classroom teacher, who had no background in drama, and her thirty-two students of mixed ethnic and academic backgrounds. The experience was documented by filmmaker Peggy Stern, who ultimately made a twenty-four-minute documentary film called *Standing*

Tall (available online, with a Study Guide I wrote, through Fanlight Productions, 2004).

Throughout the process, all involved not only planned and executed the dramatizations, but also reflected together upon the process. The drama therapist asked the children at the conclusion of each of fifteen sessions what they had learned from the day's work and how the fictional characters and themes related to their own lives. Following that, the drama therapist, teacher, and teaching artist met to evaluate the session, engaging in a critical dialogue about the moments of forward and backward movement, about when and how to move from the fictional Standing Tall to the actual New York City, about how to dramatize charged figures like Osama bin Laden, about stereotyping and scapegoating, about when to poke fun and when to be serious, about how to help children and adults alike make sense of a senseless act of terror, about when to move from drama to theatre, from improvisation to formal performance, about how to juggle the needs and expectations of administrators, funders, filmmakers, teachers, parents, children, theatre artists, and drama therapists. Even the filmmaker engaged with the team, offering her thoughts on how to shape and highlight the process, offering questions that further challenged all involved.

At the end of these very fruitful discussions, the team prepared for the following week. Through this reflective process, the collaborators evaluated the week's work and assessed the needs of the children and of each other, looking especially for moments that both did and did not enhance the educational and therapeutic experience of the players. Although no definitive answers were given to the most complex questions, the group proceeded on to performance, which was attended not only by the school community but also by parents and friends of the children. During a talkback discussion with the audience directly following the play, many older children and adults said that this moment was the first time they had the opportunity to speak about their own experiences during 9/11 and to begin to make some meaning of that day.

The results of an evaluative questionnaire circulated to the parents of the children involved affirmed that the Standing Tall experience did indeed help the children begin to put some degree of closure on the experience. In the film, one philosophical ten-year-old girl reflects upon the full experience: "The drama class pretty much changed my life... I don't know what I'd do (without this experience)... I'd be dead in my mind."

As a model of action, reflection and transformation (see Taylor, 2003), and of assessment and evaluation within a dialogical process, the Standing Tall experience was highly effective.

At some point in the foreseeable future, at a time when boundaries between academic disciplines are more permeable, arts-based assessors might find ways to link measures developed in discrepant arenas. It may well be desirable for drama teachers and drama therapists to learn from each other. The generic in both fields is performance, the act of telling a story in role to some real or imagined audience for some discernible purpose. In that all applied drama/theatre practitioners are concerned with the applications of performance to learning and to human growth and development, then the major blocks to this dialogue are in the minds of the practitioners and the administrators who support them.

Applied drama and theatre is not quite a formal discipline, although it is on its way (see Taylor, 2003). When it fully arrives, it would be of great benefit to its consumers if all concerned—teachers and therapists, community leaders, teaching artists, administrators, and supervisors—would look toward ways of embracing the learning and healing process by developing optimal assessments and evaluations.

In the dawn of educational drama, as educators skilled in the art form of drama/theatre were developing approaches and rationales for applying the art form to the education of their students, it was important to establish a discipline separate from the art of theatre. And in the dawn of drama therapy, as therapists skilled in applying dramatic approaches and theories to human development and remediation developed their craft, it was important to establish a discipline separate from both theatre and educational drama. These two applied areas are now established, with many subsets such as Theatre-in-Education, theatre for development, children's theatre, youth theatre, theatre of the oppressed, playback theatre, and psychodrama. Given this plethora of unique dramatic approaches, isn't it time to look at the common performance source from which all these specialties emerged?

An assumption that pervades this chapter is that, yes, it is time to engage in productive dialogue among the various subspecializations of applied drama. There is a new generation of practitioners and thinkers in both educational drama and theatre and drama therapy prepared to do so. They face many challenges—a history marked by struggles for acceptance and resources, a current conservative economic and political climate of diminishing financial support for subject matter without a clear, quantitative research base, a psychology of being perceived as less than those in the art form itself, and a poor track record of building bridges to others in related fields. Given these challenges, and assessing the benefits of building the appropriate bridges, applied drama practitioners can move forward, one step at a time.

In a time of cutbacks and accountability, when redundancies are carefully scrutinized and administrators are mandated to reduce faculty and practitioners in nonessential fields, it is indeed time to work together. Assessment and evaluation can become rallying points for this long overdue collaboration. Imagine how much more powerful a university-based program in applied drama could be if it fostered an ongoing dialogue among drama teachers, teaching artists, drama therapists, puppeteers, psychodramatists, community drama specialists, children and youth theatre specialists, and TIE practitioners. Through that dialogue, projects could be launched that address the most pressing social, political, economic, and cultural issues of our time or, indeed, any time. Through that dialogue, a research agenda could be launched that looks at multiple methodologies and procedures essential in validating the outcomes of education and treatment of a range of individuals through drama.

And imagine a K–12 school-based drama program that included input from many of the applied drama practitioners and theorists mentioned above. Such a program would be sensitive to the dramatic education of individuals in terms of their affective, cognitive, psychomotor, social, aesthetic, and spiritual development. Collaborators in such a program would be capable of devising assessment and evaluation instruments that draw from a broad understanding of performance and its vicissitudes.

Throughout the twentieth century and into the twenty-first, many men and women of vision have discovered ways to enhance the quality of life of students and those in need of therapy through an application of the art form of drama/theatre. Many, by necessity, have made their discoveries in isolation of related fields and of the larger field of drama/theatre and the even larger arenas of arts, education, and psychotherapy. It is time to move out of that splendid isolation. It is time to say: "We are ready. We have the knowledge and the will and the security to share our knowledge and our resources as a means to make the optimal impact upon our students, patients, clients, consumers." If arts-based assessments are shared, the field of assessment becomes the richer. Those to be assessed will benefit and those assessing will be challenged to move into new territory that further reveals the power of their work.

WORKS CITED

Bloom, B., D. Krathwohl, and B. Masia. 1956. *Taxonomy of Educational Objectives, Handbook I: Cognitive Domain*. New York: David McKay.

Bolton, G. 1984. *Drama as Education*. London: Longman.

Brissett, D., and C. Edgley (eds.) 1975. *Life as Theatre: A Dramaturgical Sourcebook*. Chicago: Aldine.

Buck, J. 1966. *The House-Tree-Person Technique: Revised Manual*. Beverly Hills, CA: Western Psychological Services.

Burke, K. 1972. *Dramatism and Development*. Barre, MA: Clark University Press.

Cook, C. 1917. *The Play Way*. London: Heinemann.

Cooley, C. 1922. *Human Nature and Social Order*. New York: Scribner's.

Courtney, R. 1973. Drama and Pedagogy. In *Discussions in Developmental Drama 10*. University of Calgary, 56–57.

———. 1974. *Play, Drama and Thought*. New York: Drama Books Specialists.

Dewey, J. 1966. *Democracy and Education*. New York: Free Press.

Elin, N., and A. Nucho. 1979. "The Use of Kinetic Family Drawing as a Diagnostic Tool in Assessing the Child's Self-concept." *Art Psychotherapy*, 6: 241–47.

Gersie, A. 1991. *Storymaking in Bereavement*. London: Jessica Kingsley.

———. 1997. *Reflections on Therapeutic Storymaking*. London: Jessica Kingsley.

Goffman, E. 1959. *The Presentation of Self in Everyday Life*. Garden City, New York: Doubleday.

Hornbrook, D. 1998. *Education and Dramatic Art*. 2d ed. London: Routledge.

James, M. and D. R. Johnson. 1997. "Drama Therapy in the Treatment of Combat-related Post-traumatic Stress Disorder." *The Arts in Psychotherapy*, 23(5): 383–95.

Jennings, S. 1997. *Introduction to Dramatherapy: Ariadne's Ball of Thread*. London: Jessica Kingsley.

Johnson, D. R. 1988. "The Diagnostic Role-playing Test." *The Arts in Psychotherapy*, 15, 1:23–36.

Johnson, D. R., and D. Quinlan. 1993. "Can the Mental Representations of Paranoid Schizophrenics Be Differentiated from Those of Normals?" *Journal of Personality Assessment*, 60, 588–601.

Johnson, L., and C. O'Neill (eds.) 1991. *Collected Writings on Education and Drama/Dorothy Heathcote*. Evanston, IL: Northwestern University Press.

Kohl, H. 1970. *The Open Classroom: A Practical Guide to a New Way of Teaching*. New York: Vintage Books.

Laban, R. 1960. *The Mastery of Movement*. London: Macdonald and Evans.

Lahad, M. 1992. "Storymaking: An Assessment Method of Coping with Stress." In *Dramatherapy, Theory and Practice 2.* S. Jennings, ed. London: Routledge.

Landy, R. 1975. *Dramatic Education: An Interdisciplinary Approach to Learning.* Unpublished Ph.D. dissertation, University of California, Santa Barbara.

———. 1993. *Persona and Performance—The Meaning of Role in Drama, Therapy and Everyday Life.* New York: Guilford.

———. 1994. *Drama Therapy: Concepts, Theories and Practices.* Springfield, IL: Charles C. Thomas.

———. 1996. *Essays in Drama Therapy: The Double Life.* London: Jessica Kingsley.

———. 2000. "Role Theory and the Role Method of Drama Therapy." In *Current Approaches in Drama Therapy.* P. Lewis and D. R. Johnson, eds. Springfield, IL: Charles C. Thomas.

———. 2001a. "Tell-A-Story—A New Assessment in Drama Therapy." In *New Essays in Drama Therapy—Unfinished Business.* R. Landy, ed. Springfield, IL: Charles C. Thomas.

——— 2001b. "Role Profiles—An Assessment Instrument." In *New Essays in Drama Therapy—Unfinished Business.* R. Landy, ed. Springfield, IL: Charles C. Thomas.

Landy, R., B. Luck, E. Conner, and S. McMullian. 2003. "Role Profiles: A Drama Therapy Assessment Instrument." *The Arts in Psychotherapy,* 30, (3): 151–61.

Manley, J., et. al. 1971. *Drama/Theatre Framework for California Public Schools.* Sacramento: California State Department of Education.

Maslow, A. 1963. *Toward a Psychology of Being.* Princeton, NJ: Nostrand.

Marcuse, H. 1972. *Counterrevolution and Revolt.* Boston: Beacon Press.

New York State Learning Standards for the Arts. 1996. Online. http://www.emsc.nysed.gov/ciai/arts/pub/artlearn.pdf.

Perls, F. 1969. *Gestalt Therapy Verbatim.* Moab, UT: Real People Press.

Pestalozzi, H. 1951. *The Education of Man.* New York: Greenwood Press.

Piaget, J. 1962. *Play, Dreams and Imitation in Childhood.* New York: Norton.

Polanyi, M. 1966. *The Tacit Dimension.* Garden City, NY: Doubleday.

Rogers, C. 1961. *On Becoming a Person.* Boston: Houghton Mifflin.

Shaw, A. 1970. "A Taxonomical Study of the Nature and Behavioral Objectives of Creative Dramatics." *Educational Theatre Journal,* 22: 361–72.

Slade, P. 1954. *Child Drama.* London: University Press.

Taylor, P. 2003. *Applied Theatre: Creating Transformative Encounters in the Community.* Portsmouth: Heinemann.

Ward, W. 1930. *Creative Dramatics.* New York: Appleton-Century-Crofts.

Way, B. 1967. *Development Through Drama.* London: Longman.

Wilshire, B. 1982 *Role Playing and Identity: The Limits of Theatre as Metaphor.* Bloomington: Indiana University Press.

Chapter 6

Returning the Aesthetic to the Theatre/Drama Classroom

Philip Taylor

Anal probes
Lock step
Cookie Cutter
MCAS
Question
Pressure Point
Imagination

So begins the opening to a new drama, *Ah—Ssess* exploring the dogged and perennial issue of assessment and evaluation. Presented at the International Drama in Education Research Institute, and the NYU Forum on Assessment in Arts Education, *Ah—Ssess* was a script powered by the voices of educators, administrators, parents, and schoolchildren who were grappling with the Massachusetts Comprehensive Assessment System, otherwise known as MCAS. Six actors represented the multiple perspectives and varying positions school communities and their administrations face when making determinations about human achievement and progress in an MCAS era. These ranged from the rigid evaluation structures imposed on teachers, the obsession with rubrics and other criterion-based reporting, to the difficulties of finding appropriate and useful descriptors when assessing artistic development (Taylor, 2004, 24).

While *Ah—Ssess* puts a human face to the hopes and struggles of classroom teachers who are challenged daily with large classes, fewer preparation periods, and an ever-increasing administration trail, it was not able to present any satisfying solutions as to how educators balance the external pressures to deliver a prescribed program of study with their own understanding of what is valuable and worth knowing. Indeed, *Ah—Ssess* presented quite a devastating portrait of faceless teachers who have sold their souls to the MCAS, or who feel powerless to realize their aesthetic vision.

In the previous chapter, Robert Landy highlighted many of the patterns and developments in theatre education assessment. It is indeed the case that assessment has been a complex issue in the field, and the various disparate positions people have on this topic are largely based on the particular educational drama philosophy to which they subscribe. In the United States, the movement known as creative drama, as espoused by Winifred Ward at Northwestern University from the 1930s (1930, 1957), is still influential with those who commit to nonscripted collaborative enactment in classrooms. Ward, influenced by Dewey (1921) and Mearns (1958) argued that creative drama developed the whole person in that it benefited children's physical, intellectual, social, and emotional welfare. At New York University, for instance, Nellie McCaslin, faculty member for over thirty years, was a strong advocate of the Ward approach, introducing numerous courses in this method. McCaslin's text *Creative Drama in the Classroom and Beyond* was released in its eighth edition in 2005, just after her death, and is possibly one of the most popular selling texts in the U.S. field today.

The creative drama practitioner adopted a linear approach to lesson planning and usually designed a sequential series of activities children would typically encounter: "the sequence proceeds from sensory/concentration activities to movement/pantomime, dialogue, characterization, and improvisation/story playing" (Wright, 1985, 205). Students would often reenact story plots, cast the narrative, open the props cupboard, and utilize whatever resources they could. Following the enactment, the group would evaluate their efforts: "the building of the play demands keen thought and imagination, for it must be orderly, reasonable, convincing, permitting of no slipshod thinking and imagining" (1930, 30). Reading this description today we are left wondering what precisely characterizes "slipshod thinking and imagining." A critical theorist might suggest there is an underlying agenda here, serving the heteronormative status quo.

Nonetheless, the pedagogy emphasized the skill and talent that children could bring to their creative play: "characterization, development of plot, enriching of dialogue and action, ensemble work, and tempo are to be emphasized in class critique, with voice and diction understood to be vitally important" (46). While the educational premise informing the rhetoric was based on releasing the imagination, an informal checklist of external outcomes that teachers should seek was still operating. I wonder what creative drama leaders understood by the phrase "keen thought and imagination," as the term was never fully explained, and appeared to be essentially powered by subjective interpretations. Many of the U.S. dissertations that have researched drama in the curriculum have shown that Ward's pedagogy is the predominant mode in which teachers have worked (see Wagner, 1998, for examples of these studies).

Not all devotees of educational drama and theatre in the classroom have been aficionados of the Ward method. Landy has identified some of these movements, including child drama (Slade, 1954) and developmental drama (Way, 1967), each with its own particular emphases and orientations (see Taylor, 2000). Nonetheless, whatever movement or philosophy was the influence, there was still a strong emphasis of theatre production in schools. The United States has not had the same fierce debates concerning process and product that dominated conferences in England and Canada throughout most of the 1970s and 1980s. However, when British pioneer Dorothy Heathcote landed on American soil in 1969 to speak at Northwestern University, the institution where Ward herself had taught, the creative drama movement was rocked, as were the dominant beliefs concerning assessment.

Heathcote (1967) challenged theatre educators to go back to basic principles: What is drama? Why art? For Heathcote, the focus on reenactments, and the concern with pursuing linear narratives, did not strike her as aesthetically resonant:

> Dramatic improvisation is concerned with what we discover for ourselves and the group when we place ourselves in a human situation containing some element of desperation. Very simply it means putting yourself into other people's shoes and, by using personal experience

to help you to understand their point of view, you may discover more than you knew when you started. (44)

She believed in thoughtfully structured artistic experiences where the stakes were raised as students adopted roles and attitudes. Drama, in her mind, focused on people involved in challenging situations, usually facing a dilemma, and drawing on their own resources to get out of the "mess" in which they found themselves. This might be a group of children recreating the American pioneers settling in rugged country, say, or a group of scientists looking to cure cancer. In both instances, the group is endowed with a role and a task, and they encounter numerous obstacles on their journey. Process drama, as her genre of drama praxis became known, required participants to explore events, issues, ideas and relationships.

Heathcote had a unique gift of understanding the elements of drama, and how playwrights crafted tales and lured their audiences into imaginary worlds. Her praxis required that the dramatist's palette needed to be adopted by teachers, and that educators should get in touch with their own aesthetic sensibility. Aesthetic, in Heathcote's mind, required students to operate in two different worlds: the fictitious and the real. It envisaged heightening students' critical and perceptual powers when deconstructing and reflecting. Most particularly, she was interested in the semiotics of theatre, how actors sign, and how spectators read those signs. Not interested in simplistic responses to complex issues, she invited classes to tolerate the ambiguity of a dramatic encounter, and to embrace complexity and multiplicity (see Bolton, 2003, for a full description of Heathcote's aesthetic). Intuitive and extrinsic knowledge of dramatic form was central in this praxis. She introduced many role and distancing conventions, especially the teacher in role, that would help establish an imaginary world. In this respect, quite a different conception of the teacher's function was envisaged: from facilitator or instructor, to a collaborator and coartist.

This notion of a grounded aesthetic sensibility, laden with contextual value, privileged the participants' experience and became considerably influential in the 1960s and 1970s, as teachers jointly devised with their students improvised scenarios exploring the human condition. In the United States, this work went hand in hand with a formal study of theatre in the classroom. Advocates of the

Heathcotean process-drama approach became critical of evaluation models that prioritized traditional instruction in theatre skills and content; and which deskilled students' perceptual abilities (Bolton, 1998; O'Toole, 1992; Taylor and Warner, 2006; Wilhelm and Edmiston, 1998; Wagner, 1999). While clearly a theatre curriculum needs to develop students' understanding of dramatic form, and its adept manipulation, with accompanying study in theatre evolution and criticism, script analysis, and play production, the movement known as "outcome-based learning" undermined teachers interested in process.

An outcomes orientation emphasizes students' content knowledge of plays, movements, skills, and technologies. Teachers become relegated to the role of an evaluator who critiques whether the students are regurgitating the perceived wisdom on what people should know and be able to do in the arts. Heathcotean process drama could not easily fit into the so-called checklist of external attainment given the former's interest with how students were transacting with an arts experience, what we might characterize as the qualitative encounter. There has been a gradual diminution of process-oriented approaches in the drama classroom, and an infatuation with the quantitative.

PRESSURE POINTS: BRING ON EVALUATION

The idea that teachers are now assessing students' learning is clearly a misnomer. Assessment has generally referred to the ongoing monitoring of how teachers and students are managing a particular task. Assessment was crucial in a process drama encounter, as teachers needed to read in action whether the group understood the logic of, say, an improvised scenario, whether they were able to build belief, and how well their sense of dramatic form led to satisfying encounters. Assessment is helpful to teachers as they can review how their own decision-making shapes the quality of the work. Likewise, students benefited from having their reflective capabilities heightened. Students who were challenged to take on a role, or struggled to find ways of developing the drama in role, or who were simply unsure of what was required in a particular dramatic context, could consult with their compatriots, and try out different approaches. This ability to reflect in and on action is pivotal to teachers' and students' ability to develop and refine their perceptual tastes. Such experimentation, or trial and improvement, had been the linchpin of the theatre curriculum.

A sole focus on outcomes, however, does not help teachers trust in their own voices to probe with their students, to review, to try out, and experiment. Outcome-oriented teachers usually forget that the human context shapes the theatre classroom, and they become driven to evaluate end products. When we work in role in process drama or as we develop character in theatre production, we are bringing our own bodies and minds to that creative process. In order to create and perform satisfying theatre, we need to be in touch with how our bodies work as communicative systems. We need to understand the power of voice, space, time, gesture. We need to become adept at sculpting resonant images. We need to have a grasp of the various dramatic genres and styles, where and how they emerged, and when we might incorporate them into our dramatic vocabulary. We have to develop theatre literacy beyond just a rote-learning approach where we parrot off the standard classics or the familiar technical jargon. In other words, the theatre educator has to assess whether our students have acquired an aesthetic sensibility, and if they haven't, then teachers need to reassess their curriculum and make the necessary adjustments.

Fortunately, there are a few authors who remind us that a social contract operates in the drama classroom, and that the success of our work is dependent on the relationships that are built between teachers and the students. In my experience working in American, Australian, and British schools, the most successful teachers are those who endeavor to read and respond to the human dimension. Such educators are dedicated to their craft and have a love for their work, and are able to find ways of remaining true to their own artistic pedagogy while satisfying the external mandates. Interestingly, many of these current authors are working in, or writing about drama in the elementary classroom, where the pressures to focus on outcomes, for the moment at least, are not as prominent as in the secondary school.

"To ensure a balanced evaluation," write O'Toole and Dunn (2002), "we should consider how effectively students organize, manage, construct, express and reflect *throughout* their drama activities" (my emphasis, 25). Good evaluation then has to include progressive assessments by the teachers and their students. O'Toole and Dunn offer some useful questions for educators to consider:

- What do I want the students to know/do?
- Are the students working effectively within the dramatic context? Do they understand the dramatic contract and can they sustain involvement?

- Do the students handle the content of the drama appropriately? Are they understanding the context and learning about its implications?
- Are they able to cope with the linguistic and kinesthetic demands placed on them?
- How effectively do the students use the medium of drama? Are they managing the elements of drama comfortably and with skill?
- Are the children able to interact and learn socially through the group process? Do they show a willingness to work with a wide range of people; work confidently in pairs, small groups, or large groups; show tolerance for the ideas, feelings, and attitudes of others; solve problems through negotiation?
- Are the children able to take some responsibility, first, for their own work and, second, for the class or group drama work? Do they take on a variety of roles including leadership and support as required within the drama?
- Are they able to reflect? Do they make comments about their own progress, offer appropriate developments of the drama and new initiatives? (26)

Within this framework, the teacher is operating as a participant-observer, stepping in and out of the work, noticing how the participants are engaging with the drama and what they are learning. I like these questions because they emphasize tracking the students' interest in making drama, their willingness to present drama, and to reflect both on and in the dramatic process. The first question, *What do I want the students to know/do?* is critical, as it anticipates that there is an aesthetic imperative that a teacher believes will provide an important scaffold. So often, it seems to me, teachers really don't know what they want to do, or have lacked confidence in their own ability to structure a significant drama experience. They think in terms of discrete unit or lesson plans, isolated modules and study programs, with neither internal nor interrelated coherence. They also neglect to recognize that ultimately they are presenting themselves, their loves and passions, their personal aesthetic. You are what you teach, not a series of bulleted points under a discrete attainment target.

Equally though we need to find ways of asking students to reflect on their own evolving aesthetic, and that of their fellow students. "Self assessment and peer assessment are two other important evaluation tools," write O'Toole and Dunn, that can be adapted. When students feel that their own critical responses are being included, it is inevitable that they will have more ownership of the material:

> Self-assessment, in the form of a journal or diary, can be a very effec-
> tive means of gaining the reflective qualities that we seek in our stu-
> dents. . . The comments of peers can also be appropriately applied,
> with students asked to respond to the work of their classmates.
> Again, this form of evaluation extends reflective skills and can
> enhance the cohesion of the group. (28)

We cannot separate assessment and evaluation from the learning experiences. There is always going to be product in process, and process in product. I don't want to put up a binary of formative and summative in this chapter, but clearly the teacher is endeavoring to collect data from a variety of different sources: through observation, through the students' responses and their ability to manipulate the theatrical canvass, through the portfolios and reflections that students maintain. Indeed, teachers are constantly searching for multiple ways in which students can demonstrate their relationship to the curriculum, so that often the formative collapses into the summative, and vice versa.

In this participant-observer model, educators are rethinking their plans in action, because they recognize the social context of the drama. The human dimension in the drama classroom, as good teachers know, can shape what is possible, and what is not. In a rich, three-year longitudinal study on drama in the elementary school curriculum in England, it was found that you cannot separate social learning from artistic learning. Both are connected and must be recognized in any successful assessment model. While the five assessment principles below were generated from this British study, they clearly relate to the argument I am putting forward here:

Five Assessment Principles

1. Pupils should be provided with a range of opportunities to demonstrate their abilities in different ways, and through different situations across the key stages.
   (*Note:* Key stages in England refer to levels of achievement.)

2. Assessment should be promoted as a form of personalized learning, used to raise self-esteem and motivate pupils through the teaching and learning.
3. Pupils should be actively involved in their own learning; opportunities and strategies should be created for pupils to assess themselves and each other in order to understand how they can build on and improve their own practice.
4. Activities should be created to address "gaps" in pupils' understanding.
5. Planning should include selecting from a range of teaching styles to differentiate and/or personalize learning and to enhance progression.

(R. Dickinson, J. Neelands, and Shenton School, 2006, 143).

The learning opportunities that teachers provide, which includes activating the students' capacity to join in the assessment experience, builds rich communities of inquiry.

One challenge with the outcomes approach is that it places more emphasis on the propositional knowledge the students regurgitate than on what the teachers are actually doing at any particular time. Ackroyd and Boutlon (2001) claim that the most satisfying learning experiences in drama operate when the teachers are flexible, imaginative, able to think on their feet and take a risk Regrettably, many curriculum guides do not emphasize how the teachers' implementation of drama education impacts on the learning encounter.

Again, it seems to me, at the core of a satisfying assessment model is the teacher's ability to address the questions Heathcote posed: Why drama? Why art? Time and again I go into classrooms where there does not seem to be an aesthetic principle shaping the classroom experience. Fleming (2001) agrees:

> If a concept of aesthetic education is to make any sense, it is imperative that as teachers we attend to the nature of the experience which the pupils are having. Not to do so will be accepting that a valid drama experience will be had by pupils who are merely mouthing lines without any understanding and engagement, or mindlessly painting scenery without any sense of meaning and purpose. To accept this view is to return to practices which drama teachers have sought to escape from for 50 years. (60)

Nonetheless, the influx of technocratic models, which I explore in the next section, is preventing teachers from realizing their own artistic impulses. Appeals to "restore the dramatic product to a central position," to teach students "what they need to be taught," and to promote "attainment targets" are forever in our midst, and seem to emerge from a high-art, and culturally elite position (Hornbrook, quoted in Taylor, 2000). One author writes of the need to set quantifiable outputs, where students "are not assessed on their private values, beliefs or attitudes, but on their actual and visible contributions to the development and realization of the drama" (Nicholson, 2000, 15). But both the actor on stage, and the child in an improvised school drama, are drawing on their inner landscape as they create role. Whether a grade ten student inhabits a character from a Brecht play, or a third grader is exploring the position of the wolf in *The Three Little Pigs*, it is the subjective interpretation of those roles, based on life experiences, that shapes the dramatic context. To focus alone on the *actual and visible* undermines the complex inter- and intrapersonal processes that fuel a drama encounter.

THE TECHNOCRAT—ANAL PROBING THE CURRICULUM

The need to have a fixed reality where outcomes can be predicted in advance and where human growth can be tabulated via taxonomy of competencies is not new. We attribute that form of knowing driven by the empirical sciences to the movement of positivism, which articulated that there were objective and unambiguous readings of the world. Comte (1848/1910), the founder of this philosophy, claimed there are particular (actual and visible) ways the world can be read, and theories that can be deduced based upon the known and the real. As metaphysical substances are not real, social scientists "should limit themselves to particular data as a factual source out of which experimentally valid laws can be derived" (Christians, 2005, 143). We can only know what we see, not what we can imagine, and therefore scientific knowledge must be privileged. In this respect, the role of schools is to deliver information and skills that will allow us to achieve technical competency through which we can become so-called productive members of the community.

Here, there is an emphasis on abilities and talents that need to be taught, usually according to a predetermined and standardized curriculum package. But, as Kincheloe (2005) reminds us, such documents rarely take into account "issues of complexity" like the following:

- The ambiguity of language and its less-than-transparent meanings
- The ways individual minds rarely perceive phenomena and their meanings in the same way
- Meaning-making is not simply a rational process
- The boundary between rationality and irrationality is blurred
- The construction of a neutral curriculum is an impossibility
- Researchers coming from different value positions will produce often contradictory information about a particular artifact or text
- The nature of the disagreements about the benefits of Western reason (109)

Often, published curriculum resources do not activate teachers' professional competence in making educational decisions concerning their own students. Technocratic imperatives rarely cater to individual student differences or classroom context. They often reinforce white, heteronormative, socially mobile, and phallocentric ideology. The instructional handbooks generalize across class and population, and teachers usually have had no input into the content generation. The teachers' obligation is to moderate within the framework, forget they have any counter ideas, and hope their students achieve well on the tests.

Claims that theatre teachers need to embrace a subject-orientated approach, rather than a pedagogical one, become the cherished ideals for the technocrat. One writer asserts that such alone will restore dramatic art to the classroom, where its "curriculum" can be "practiced, developed, and taught" (Hornbrook, 1998, 132). The textbook and the publishing house become central to the training of teachers and students. Knowledge has to be transmittable and curriculum prescribed:

By the age of 11 in drama most students should be able to make and take part in improvised scenes and act out convincing characters. They should also have developed sufficient physical flexibility to enable them to adapt voice and movement in a controlled manner to the characters they play.

By this age, students should have grasped the principles which govern the creation of a dramatic environment and be aware of the potential use of design and technology in drama. . . At 11, most students in drama should be able to expand scenarios into simple dramatic scripts. By the time they leave the primary school, all students should know how to polish their work for presentation and should have become accustomed to the disciplines of rehearsal and to the process of refining their plays in the light of audience response (Hornbrook, 1991, 133–34)

There is a tension between education and training in this model, for education has tended to refer to the process of drawing out knowledge from within, whereas training focuses on delivering information within confined structures, delimiting knowledge to set boundaries and controls. In the above account, it seems bizarre that terms like "convincing characters," "sufficient physical flexibility," "be aware of the potential," "polish their work," and "become accustomed to" are used as though there is some agreed-upon understanding of such value-laden terms. Surely students' physical flexibility is determined by what their bodies can actually do? And what does it mean for eleven-year-olds "to polish their work for presentation." Again, notions of "polish" would have to be informed by the classroom context, the students' capability and the task at hand. These determinations by teachers are always going to be subjectively informed anyway. No matter what standards or outcomes one has, two teachers working from the same curriculum, with the same class, are inevitably going to have different interpretations of what a polished presentation looks like. Positivist obsessiveness is perilous to the arts. It neutralizes the curriculum and denies ambiguous, shifting, or contradictory readings of the world.

It saddens me when I go into British high school classrooms now, mainly in London, and see this maddening obsession with benchmarking and attainment targets. It also appears that no drama textbook will ever get published there unless it is tied into the national curriculum. "Since the introduction of the National Curriculum (NC) we have witnessed fundamental changes in the structure and content of the curriculum," argue Toye and Prendville (2000). The "new demands" in "assessment, recording and reporting of pupils' progress," they suggest, lead to an infatuation with accountability that "has never been greater" (7).

Accountable to whom? one might ask, the teachers, their students? No, to OFSTED (Office for Standards in Education), what I liken to the Big Brother of British education. Go into a London classroom, and you will inevitably see a notice from OFSTED pinned to the walls with anxious-looking teachers awaiting the visit from the OFSTED inspectorate:

> The prescriptive nature of the curriculum is not without its critics. Initially the NC was over-complex and unmanageable, and more recently it has been largely assessment-driven. There is also the added pressure of published league tables for schools as well as published OFSTED reports following school inspections. The allocation of time to the literacy and numeracy hours necessitates an "efficient" delivery of the curriculum so that it can maintain the prerequisite of "breadth and balance." (7)

For years, England was the inspiration for countries worldwide, known for its transformative process drama work, inspired by the brilliance of such leaders as Ackroyd (2000), Bolton (1998), Heathcote (1967), Neelands (1984), and O'Neill (1995). In their aesthetic, the valuing of the student stance was crucial to the teacher's planning. Teachers were able to rethink plans in action, and skip off the page when the students pursued an unforeseen direction. Now, however, we find an emphasis on conservative teaching instruction in classic script-based study, with conventional lessons on play production, semiotic analysis of text, and theatre history and development. It seems that we can no longer look to our friends over the Atlantic for innovation.

So what do we find when we investigate closer to home? Regrettably, the technocrat is in full swing here: there is a plethora of federal and state policies, curriculum frameworks, and blueprints that govern what happens in schools, the Massachusetts Comprehensive Assessment System (MCAS) being just one such indicator. When the teachers in the *Ah—Ssess* script kept referring to the menace of MCAS, they were typically reiterating their sense of hopelessness and despair.

MCAS claims there are generic human competencies that can be measured against a checklist. Note the tone of the MCAS description below with its emphasis on testing, administering, measuring, reporting. There is clearly an impersonal attitude that shapes the technocratic approach, and that consequently disempowers teachers to believe in their own ability to shape and influence the curriculum. MCAS was implemented in response to the Education Reform Law of 1993, which required that it be designed to:

- Test all public school students across the Commonwealth, including students with disabilities and students with limited English proficiency

- Be administered annually in selected grades
- Measure performance based on the learning standards in the Massachusetts Curriculum Frameworks
- Report on the performance of individual students, schools, and districts
- Serve as one basis of accountability for students, schools, and districts (for example, grade ten students must pass the MCAS tests as one condition of eligibility for earning a high school diploma)

In addition to meeting the requirements of the Education Reform Law, the MCAS tests also fulfill the requirements of the federal No Child Left Behind (NCLB) law. NCLB requires annual assessments in reading and mathematics for students in grades three–eight and high school. Students also must be tested annually in science in an elementary school grade, a middle school grade, and a high school (ten–twelve) grade. This requirement is fulfilled in Massachusetts by testing students in grades five, eight, and high school (http://www.doe.mass.edu/mcas/overview_faq.html).

Nomenclature, like NCLB and MCAS, becomes the standard (like OFSTED), and before you know it these terms become acceptable vernacular and take on a life of their own. Yet, for the most part, teachers and their students have had little or anything to do with generating the knowledge that feeds into the standard. As Giroux (in Grundy, 1987) writes:

> In this view, knowledge is objective, "bounded" and "out there." Class-room knowledge is often treated as an external body of information, the production of which appears to be independent of human beings. From this perspective, human knowledge is viewed as being inde-pendent of time and place; it becomes universalized ahistorical knowl-edge. Moreover it is expressed in a language which is basically techni-cal and allegedly value free... Knowledge, then, becomes not only countable and measurable, it also becomes impersonal. Teaching in this pedagogical paradigm is usually discipline-based and treats subject matter in a compartmentalized and atomized fashion. (34)

The reality is that teachers are operating under this culture of posi-tivism every day. For the most part, they feel they have no control over their professional lives as they are constantly scrutinized and evalu-ated by others. And such evaluation is usually set against prescribed categories that the teacher has had no input in developing. And yet when some of these standards documents write of the importance of teachers becoming reflective practitioners and action researchers, it is usually for the purposes of delivering the published curriculum package more swiftly.

In theatre education we have seen how the technocratic imperative has fed into educators' planning for some years. We have witnessed a myriad of frameworks and documents that promote a view that there are clear endpoints that need to be taught. It was possibly the influential Calouste Gulbenkian Foundation's 1982 report, *The Arts in Schools: Principles, Practice and Provision*, that paved the way for a set of benchmark standards with itemized levels of achievement. The need to promote the arts in a way that sold to employers and industry was clearly articulated in the introduction to the report:

> . . .any contemporary discussion of education has to be set against the background of . . .
> a. the profound and long-term changes in the patterns of employment and of unemployment, especially among young people
> b. the changing relationships between education and society as a whole (3)

Educators feel compelled to promote the arts' economic and industry benefits, and, in doing so, they support the ever-increasing socialization of schools to achieve a government-political agenda. Profile/descriptive reporting and criterion-referenced tests become priorities as does the need to assemble a lengthy database of skills and abilities young people should demonstrate at various levels. The NCC Arts in Schools Project (1990) argued that a key assessment element required "a comparison." And this element must conform to general and agreed-upon principles:

> . . .statements of assessment should be clear about, and should state, the criteria for comparison that are being used. Is the work being compared with that of other children? With children of the same age? With the pupil's own previous work? To some view of the pupil's potential? To professional standards? . . .in doing all of this, it increases the necessary objectivity of assessment in the arts. (63)

Ah, therein lies the rub of many arts frameworks, "the necessary objectivity of assessment in the arts." Curriculum is not an active lived encounter between teacher and students, but a static implementation of externally driven competencies. How will it ever be possible for teachers and their students to develop their artistic impulses when "necessary objectivity" comes into play? Time and again I see this lack in operation, as teachers routinely work through their plans and units, without their own powering aesthetic vision shaping the process. While one might argue that the arts are richly personal perspectives on the world, and representative of complex subjective readings of one's place in it, too great an emphasis on objectivity and comparison seems to undermine the very reason for offering theatre education in the first place.

The consequence of this drive for objectivity has meant that curriculum programs are now neatly divided into generalized competencies, or What every American needs to know and be able to do in the arts. Generally these competencies are shaped around four key concepts:

1. *Theatre Making and Theatre Presenting*
   In this concept, students learn the basic template of drama. The so-called drama convention of taking on role, and being able to create imaginary worlds that manipulate time, space, and action are central. While improvisation and devised drama are important, the performance aspect is usually emphasized and students are evaluated on their ability to present convincing characters to public audiences.
2. *Theatre Skills and Technologies*
   In this concept, students learn how to work with their own bodies, and focus on the ways in which communication in drama occurs: kinesthetically, verbally, and aurally. Students focus on physical gesture and nuance, and study various dramatic genres. They explore design features, like costuming, lighting, set, and how multi- and digital media shape a theatrical statement. Students learn mime, commedia, poor theatre, and other acting and directing styles.
3. *Theatre Appreciation*
   In this concept, students study the development of theatre over time and in different historical contexts and locations. They critique plays and performances, and discover the playwrights who have influenced the evolution of a theatre aesthetic. World drama is emphasized, and students are urged to investigate non-Western traditions.

4. *Theatre in Society*
   In this concept, the ways in which theatre has helped influence cultural and civic identity is addressed. Theatre for social change, and the various offshoots of an applied or political and community theatre are considered. Students study theatre in their communities, the companies and residencies that exist, and how theatre educates.

On the face of it, such an approach to dividing up a theatre curriculum seems quite logical and beneficial. It appears balanced and informative, and indeed a number of textbooks now provide detailed lessons on how to achieve such. Alarmingly, though, the ways in which students tend to be assessed in these areas focuses on limited demonstration of their ability.

Let's take one example of how student teachers are being encouraged to set out their lesson plans and examine the assessment questions it provokes.

THE LESSON-PLANNING PRO FORMA: LOCKSTEP AND COOKIE CUTTER

I doubt that any reader of this chapter is going to argue that teachers do not need structure as they plan, implement, and assess classroom experiences. However, should that structure be so rigid that it prevents spontaneity or unpredictability? For instance, a textbook written for British student teachers in drama prescribes how a lesson plan should be set out:

Aims:
Write in the aims of the unit of work which this lesson forms a part. These aims will stay consistent throughout the unit of work and will form the basis of the assessment criteria.

Teaching objectives:
In this section of the lesson plan, you will need to write down the two or three points you intend to *teach* in this lesson in order to address the overall aims of the unit.

Learning objectives:
This indicates the two or three points the pupils will *learn* as a result of the lesson. They will echo the teaching objectives, but it is important that you indicate what they are learning in your planning so

that the relationship between teaching and learning is made explicit.

Continuity:
Note how the work in this lesson relates to previous work the group has done. This section ensures that you make connections between work they are currently undertaking and work undertaken before.

Progression:
Note what opportunities the lesson will provide for pupils in this group to progress in their knowledge and understanding and drama skills.

Program of study/examination syllabus:
If the drama undertaken in this lesson is linked to aspects of the National Curriculum, literacy framework or to an examination syllabus, you should record how the work complies with it. Be specific.

Assessment:
Record the assessment criteria for the unit of work here which will relate to this particular lesson. Briefly note what evidence of learning you will expect to see.

(Kempe and Nicholson, 2001, 67)

At first glance, this guide could appear quite reasonable, as it seems orderly and professional. But after some scrutiny note the technocratic model being reinforced in the plan, and the hidden assumptions that are being conveyed. There is a power relationship evident in what teachers *teach*, and what students *learn* (authors' emphasis retained). The teacher is the one in control of the objectives, the continuity, progression, and assessment. Teachers are told to be "consistent" to their aims, and not, we presume, deviate from them. While it could be argued there is still the possibility for students to generate their own learning objectives from this plan, in reality this seems unlikely because there is no indication that such negotiation and collaboration between leader and participants is being privileged in the plan itself.

When "sample lesson plans" are provided we observe a structure that is timed to perfection. In a session that aims, in part, to explore the physicality of poetic language, and to develop a dramatic and critical vocabulary, the role of the teacher as task master who instructs is clear (70):

1:25 Register and settle

1:30 Warm up from where they are sitting: close eyes and be aware of breathing. Now stand, find a space and focus on breathing again. Add a physical action, using just the arms, that reflects the movement of the breath in the body. Open eyes and keep action going. Add a sound that goes with the movement of the arm.

1:40 Stand in a circle: focus on breathing as a basis of sound/ voice. . .Word game/voice work—the whisper-Chinese whispers: send it around both directions until the sentence meets somewhere in the middle. How different are sentences: "The sacks in the tool shed smell like the seaside". . . .

1:50 Divide the group A/B around the circle. The poem we are dealing with is called "Hide and Seek." So think about how the words make you feel: what feelings do you associate with/go with the idea of hiding and seeking? A = "hide"; B = "seek." In a minute we listen to the words with eyes shut to concentrate on the sounds and think about how the sound affects us. . . The group not speaking should shut eyes and listen to the sounds of the words; the group speaking should concentrate on me: I will indicate with my hands when they should get louder and softer. Ask As to step forward.

2:00 Give out phrases from the poem. . .

2:05 As to teach Bs the phrase: repeat exercise.

2:10 People with same phrases pair up: find out which is the best way of saying the phrase.

2:20 Evaluate and clear up.

2:25 End of lesson.   (69–70)

A potential problem with this form of session presentation is that cocreation of the learning experience will rarely happen because it is not deliberately layered into the teacher education model. But even more problematic is the question of how would teachers know whether their class has achieved the aim of exploring the physicality of poetic language? I am not entirely certain to what this aim refers, Is poetry meant to be physical? Are the physical movements assisting the students to understand the poetry, and, if so, how? What we require is clarity in the intention, and a statement as to how and why the activities have been structured to facilitate the learning. As it is, I see no connection between exploring "the best way" of speaking a phrase from the poem with the Chinese whispers activity.

Allocating five minutes to "Evaluate and clear up" hardly seems sufficient for an analysis of how this sequence of activities logically enabled the teacher to achieve the stated aim. When the authors later write on "scripting lesson plans" I am equally concerned as to how this will empower teachers to read social context and adapt their plans based on immediate observation of students' responses. While I admire and respect the care that is being given to assisting beginning teachers to think about planning issues, I don't find the following statement conducive to good reflective teaching: ". . . in the early stages (of a teaching career) many student-teachers' plans can look rather like scripts. This shows that they have thought through exactly what they will need to say to the class" (72).

Yes, beginning teachers will know what they are going to say in advance if they have a script, but the students might as well not be present if their only function is to jump through the leader's hoops. Teacher as a traffic warden and timekeeper dumbs down the curriculum. There are no opportunities for deviating from the plan, no time to probe with the students what their relationship is to the material. Such a dramatic structuring is monologic; it is solely about the teacher's play. While it is clearly important for beginning teachers to have prompts, it is hard to see how our students are ever going to develop their own aesthetic vision when they feel dictated to and aren't invited to negotiate the curriculum.

QUESTION, DIALOGUE, AND IMAGINATION: DEVELOPING A CRITICAL AESTHETIC

The lockstep and cookie cutter era we are living in has arisen because teachers are no longer active producers of knowledge, but driven to achieve nebulous outputs with no rhyme or reason. We need to find more artful ways in which our lesson plans can permit students to negotiate work in process, and thereby take ownership of it. Theatre curriculum should not be presented as a series of discrete uncontested activities. If pro forma lesson plans are to be designed, and promoted, then teachers should be invited to problematize material with their students, so that knowledge can be generated in the classroom, not just transmitted. Questions inviting students in as coleaders of the learning experience are one approach. In the physical theatre example, above, questions and comments like the following could be offered throughout the session:

- What are you discovering about physicalization of the words in this poem?
- How does our focus on breathing assist in the physicalization?
- Please share with us a breathing exercise you know of that might help us engage with the poetic language.
- What skills are required to play the Chinese Whispers activity? Are there adjustments we could make to this game?
- Which words in the poem seem easy to physicalize? Which don't?
- Can you think of others words, not in the poem, that the poet might have used?
- Can we break into groups and experiment with different ways in which the poem could be said? How do those differences make an impression on the actor and audience? Create your own poems as the basis for physical theatre.
- Name some physical theatre performers. How might they approach this material? What stereotypes are associated with physical theatre? How might we challenge these?
- What are some of the challenges in the physical theatre?
- If you were teaching the class, how might you change some of the activities so that your learning was enhanced? How might physical theatre aid your direction of a play?
- What are we learning about physical theatre and dramatic form? What questions have been generated for you from this experience? Where do we go from here?

A teacher stance that does not invite students to heighten their critical faculties is not permitting the evolution of an individual and group aesthetic. When Kincheloe (2005) and other critical theorists write on the importance of dialectical authority, they are appealing for liberating educational assessments that shift the onus from teachers who deliver, to students who create. Such a stance requires regular opportunities for classroom communities to reflect in and on action:

> The authority of the critical teacher is dialectical; as teachers relinquish the authority of truth providers, they assume the mature

authority of facilitators of student inquiry and problem posing. In relation to such teacher authority, students gain their freedom—they gain the ability to become self-directed human beings capable of producing their own knowledge. (17)

The theatre classroom is a rich site for critical inquiry. It is powered by human context where students are constantly reflecting and transforming. Such articulation needs to be made more explicit in our assessments. While the current educational focus is obsessed with outcomes, teachers need to be resourceful and check in regularly with how their students are developing their own grounded aesthetic. Eisner (1985) claims "knowing the outcome of the game tells you nothing about how it is played" (141). Teachers need to ask in their classrooms, What is happening now? rather than, What is happening next? The first question requires the ability to slow down the work, deconstruct its vital characteristics, and privilege interrogation and examination of its form and content. The second question, What is happening next? reduces the curriculum to a linear, often random and illogical series of activities that serve no purpose other than time-fillers and grid completion.

If students are going to learn from their encounters with good artworks, they need to develop a conversation with them. They must experience satisfying theatre processes if they are to engage with them. Our goal as educators should be to facilitate understanding of how the arts operate as live encounters between the artist and the audience. We must not lose sight of the power of the artform to transform, to move and shift us. Action, Reflection, Transformation (ART!) are the three modalities on which good theatre education depends (Taylor, 2000). I am thinking here of the existential experience, the lived moment, the encounter between what is created and what is presented, but I am also referring to the development of an aesthetic sensibility, the perceptual ability to artfully discriminate and value what constitutes a satisfying encounter.

Teachers have to take charge of their own classrooms and activate them as sites for critical inquiry. We clearly cannot be looking for guidance from the administrators, the bureaucrats, the policy-makers; most of the current curriculum guides seem none too helpful either. They have their own agendas that, ironically in a skills-based culture, tend to deskill teachers' and students' capacity to see more clearly, and look more closely. When the classroom door is closed anything is possible, and students can be transported to imaginary worlds beyond the mechanistic tasks the handbooks offer.

In this respect, teachers need to generate their own questions about what makes a good theatre education, and enable their students, likewise, to join them in this enterprise. As Kincheloe (2005) writes:

> A vibrant professional culture depends on a group of practitioners who have the freedom to continuously reinvent themselves via their research and knowledge production. Teachers engaged in critical practice find it difficult to allow top-down content standards and their poisonous effects to go unchallenged. Such teachers cannot abide the deskilling and reduction in professional status that accompany these top-down reforms. Advocates of critical pedagogy understand that teacher empowerment does not occur just because we wish it to. Instead, it takes place when teachers develop the knowledge-work skills, the power literacy, and the pedagogical abilities befitting the calling of teaching. (19)

Fifteen years ago, almost to the day, I wrote of the perilous situation arts educators were facing given the drive toward standardization and national testing (1996). At that time, I was working in Australian higher education where national curriculum frameworks in the arts and other disciplines had been written. While that curriculum was never legislated at the federal level, the documents that were produced still largely shape how teachers think about aesthetic education today. In the United States, the No Child Left Behind law has done little to appease my concerns on how curriculum has been neutralized, denying students the opportunities to genuinely engage and build their own relationship to an aesthetic education.

Nonetheless, despair is not helpful. Historically, the arts have operated from the fringes anyway, so isolation is something we are used to, and, besides, the work has to go on. As Robert Landy reminded us in Chapter 5, theatre educators do have allies, in such fields as applied psychology, psychotherapy, anthropology, health education, and the social sciences. We need to become savvier at locating our friends and building alliances, wherever possible. But, as I have argued in this chapter, we cannot lose sight of our aesthetic imperative, and how it shapes assessment priorities, for to do so would be ultimately to sell out on our students, our art form, but most importantly, ourselves.

WORKS CITED

Ackroyd, J. 2000. *Literacy Alive!* London: Hodder and Stoughton.

Ackroyd, J., and J. Boulton. 2001. *Drama Lessons for Five- to Eleven-Year-Olds.* London: David Fulton.

Bolton, G. 1998. *Acting in Classroom Drama.* Stoke on Trent: Trentham.

————. 2003. *Dorothy Heathcote's Story: Biography of a Remarkable Drama Teacher.* Stoke on Trent: Trentham.

Calouste Gulbenkian Foundation. 1982. *The Arts in Schools: Principles, Practice and Provision.* London.

Christians, C. 2005. "Ethics and Politics in Qualitative Research." In *The Sage Handbook of Qualitative Research*, 3d ed. 139–64. Thousand Oaks: Sage.

Comte, A. 1910. *A General View of Positivism.* J. H. Bridges, trans. London: Routledge (Original work published 1848).

Dewey, J. 1921. *The School and Society.* Chicago: University of Chicago Press.

Dickinson, R., J. Neelands, and Shenton School. 2006. *Improve Your Primary School Through Drama.* London: David Fulton.

Eisner, E. 1985. *The Art of Educational Evaluation.* Philadelphia: Falmer.

Fleming, M. 2001. *Teaching Drama in Primary and Secondary Schools: An Integrated Approach.* London: David Fulton.

Grundy, S. 1987. *Curriculum: Product or Praxis.* London: Falmer.

Heathcote, D. 1967. "Improvisation." In *Dorothy Heathcote: Collected Writings on Education and Drama.* L. Johnson and C. O'Neill, eds. 44–48. London: Hutchinson.

Hornbrook, D. 1991. *Education in Drama: Casting the Dramatic Curriculum.* London: Falmer.

————. 1998. *Education and Dramatic Art*, 2d ed. London: Routledge.

Kempe, A., and H. Nicholson. 2001. *Learning to Teach Drama 11–18.* London: Continuum.

Kincheloe, J. 2005. *Critical Pedagogy Primer.* New York: Peter Lang.

McCaslin, N. 2005. *Creative Drama in the Classroom and Beyond*, 8th ed. Boston: Allyn and Bacon.

Mearns, H. 1958. *Creative Power.* 2d ed. New York: Dover.

National Curriculum Council. 1990. *The Arts 5–16: A Curriculum Framework.* Essex: Oliver and Boyd.

Neelands, J. 1984. *Making Sense of Drama.* Oxford: Heinemann.

Nicholson, H. (ed.) 2000. *Teaching Drama 11–18.* London: Continuum.

O'Neill, C. 1995. *Drama Worlds.* New Hampshire: Heinemann.

O'Toole, J. 1992. *The Process of Drama.* London: Routledge.

O'Toole, J., and J. Dunn. 2002. *Pretending to Learn: Helping Children Learn Through Drama.* Frenchs Forest, NSW, Australia: Longman.

Slade, P. 1954. *Child Drama.* London: University of London Press.

Taylor, P. (ed.) 1996. *Researching Drama and Arts Education: Paradigms and Possibilities*, London: Routledge.

————. 2000. *The Drama Classroom: Action, Reflection, Transformation*. London: RoutledgeFalmer.

————. 2004. "Qualitative Modes of Representation." *Drama Research*, 3 (June): 19–30.

Taylor, P., and C. Warner (eds). 2006. *Structure and Spontaneity*. Stoke on Trent: Trentham.

Toye, N., and F. Prendville. 2000. *Drama and the Traditional Story for the Early Years*. London: Routledge.

Wagner, B. J. 1998. *Educational Drama and Language Arts: What Research Shows*. Portsmouth: Heinemann.

————. (ed.) 1999. *Building Moral Communities through Educational Drama*. Stamford, CT: Ablex.

Way, B. 1967. *Development Through Drama*. London: Longman.

Ward, W. 1930. *Creative Dramatics*. New York: Appleton.

————. 1957. *Playmaking for Children*. New York: Appleton.

Wilhem, J., and B. Edmiston. 1998. *Imagining to Learn*. Portsmouth: Heinemann.

Wright, L. 1985. "Preparing Teachers to Put Drama in the Classroom." *Theory into Practice*, XXIV, 3:205–9.

Part IV

Visual Arts Education

Chapter 7

Embodying Visual Arts Assessment Through Touch: Imag(e)ining a Relational Arts Curriculum

Stephanie Springgay

> The work of art does not reside in the visual image, physical artifact, suggestive title or descriptive parenthetical line, but emerges in their *relational* play, a play engendered by an embodied, corporeal subject.
>
> Marsha Meskimmon, 2003 (my emphasis)

Assessment practices in both Canada and the United States raise a number of issues and concerns about learning in the visual arts. While Canada has yet to adopt national arts standards, the challenges facing both countries' visual arts curricula are embedded in debates that either view standardized assessment as depleting the arts of creativity and experimentation, or conversely are necessary in order to provide teachers with a language of practice beyond personal subjectivity and feeling, arbitrary judgments of quality, and issues of talent. Within both movements assessment is often discussed, analyzed, and implemented as distinctly separate from curriculum and pedagogy, and embedded in modernist-formalist understandings of art, art-making, and viewing. While many teachers concur that assessment of contemporary forms of art such as performance, installation, and new media art is difficult, their despair is punctured by the fact that they often attempt to "fit" postmodern practices and ways of knowing into systems of classification that are rooted in modernist understandings of art and education. Further-more, adopting or denying assessment standards does not take into consideration the complexities of gender, race, culture, ability, class, and sexuality, all components of postmodernist art education that is socially reconstructive; where art-making moves from the acquisi-tion of technical skills to a critical engagement about issues that pro-mote responsible citizenship and learning (Freedman, 2003a). In effect, assessment in the arts continues to stumble given the widen-ing split between current theories and practices within curriculum studies, and those accorded assessment. To this extent, I argue that visual arts assessment needs to be embodied and relational; recon-structed through theories of touch that challenge the mechanisms of visual perception.

In this chapter, I will critically identify some cogent issues and concerns that continue to face arts educators in the United States and Canada with respect to assessment. These complex challenges, I argue, are marked by educators' insistence on thinking of art, cur-riculum, and assessment as static and fixed, where terms like talent, creativity, and aesthetic judgment still prevail. Following this brief critical summary, I propose an embodied visual arts assessment through touch, and embed my arguments in a case study from one secondary school located in a large urban city in Canada. The posi-tion I take is to challenge arts educators to begin un/folding arts assessment as living inquiry, where the making and responding to works of art become bodied visual encounters.

ISSUES AND CONCERNS WITHIN ARTS ASSESSMENT IN CANADA AND THE UNITED STATES

Assessment in visual arts education has long been contentious. This is in part due to a belief that the arts are engaged with creativity and personal expression, and that rigorous quantifiable testing runs counter to such claims (Blaikie, 2001; Eisner, 1999). However, with increased funding cuts for arts programs, and a policy-driven movement towards standardized testing in the "core" subject areas many arts educators feel the pressure to regulate assessment (Dorn, 2003). While there is a wealth of research, literature, and opinions on visual arts assessment, the criticism of or support for assessment varies widely, illustrating the complexity of issues and concerns that arts educators face in determining the need for and implementation of assessment. Given this profusion I will focus on three issues that I believe link this comprehensive literature: (1) standardized practices universalize student performance and continue to perpetuate a mind and body split; (2) standards lead to fragmentation within curriculum and pedagogy; and (3) assessment privileges formalist understandings of art (that is, the elements and principles of design), isolating the art product as a measurement for learning and knowing.

Universalism and the Mind-Body Split

In an effort to demystify visual art and establish its worth in the curriculum alongside language arts, math, and science, visual art has often adopted standards of practice at the level of the classroom, the district, or the nation (Dorn, 2003). In the United States, such movements have included both statewide and national models—for example, *Discipline Based Art Education* (DBAE) and *Goals 2000: Education America Act* (Dorn, 2003; Hanley, 2003). The adoption of standardized practices provides art education with equality amidst the other "core" subject areas (Bensur, 2002; Boughton, et. al, 1996). Advocates of such models claim that standards impart rigor to a discipline traditionally marked by idiosyncratic practices, emotion, and subjectivity. However, while individual teachers are left with the task of adapting, modifying, and implementing them uniquely in their classrooms, the overall aim is *universalization*. Emphasis is placed on the idea that "all" students should know the same material and be able to produce specific results.

Identifying teacher reform as a possible movement towards teacher-directed change in assessment, Charles Dorn (2003) suggests that what teachers want is a single test that "can measure what students know and are able to do in all of the nation's art programs" (351). Pressing this issue further, he claims that the improbability of such a test is due in part to teachers "unwillingness" to teach art in the same way. However, as Elliot Eisner (1999) so aptly notes, the codification of standards results in an overriding assumption that one curriculum framework and one set of standards is appropriate and achievable.

Despite such audacious claims that teaching and learning should or could be presented as systematic units with codified end results, Dorn's intentions are noble, given that his response is fueled by what he sees as a pressure to regulate. This pressure, he believes, is unavoidable. Rather than presenting an alternative to universal assessment, Dorn and his coresearchers, Bob Sabol and Stan Madeja, seek authentic models of assessment that can be standardized. They argue that change needs to come from teachers, rather than mandated by external sources, a model that favors a top-down approach where teachers, and most certainly students, are last on the list of contributors and beneficiaries. "What is needed is a school authentic assessment model that involves art teachers as stakeholders in the assessment process" (Dorn, 2003, 352). While admirable, the cultivation of accountability has replaced education with schools as skill-and-knowledge factories, where learning is managed and controlled.

In Canada, Eisner's (1999) concerns that one set of standards are possible or even ethical are further problematized by the fact that not all students have equal access to arts programs "especially in elementary schools, where programs range from nonexistent to excellent" (Hanley, 2003, 35). At the secondary level, Fiona Blaikie's (2001) findings suggest that art curricula are similar, and assessment is teacher-directed and individually generated. Her study reveals that teachers and students support authentic qualitative assessment, and that teachers and students are empowered in the process.

The structure and adoption of standards, and the political pressure to demonstrate accountability in education have resulted in large-scale pencil-paper tests used by some states to determine the performance of schools. Doug Boughton (2004) criticizes such tests, which reduce knowledge to "snippets of art-related information that carry no inherent value and indicate little information about the way students make sense of their visual world" (266). The complexity of art is reduced, homogenized, and universalized through the administration of multiple-choice tests. The dilemma, Boughton argues, is to convince policy-makers that while the arts are valuable subject areas and should be assessed in conjunction with other core subject areas, the forms of assessment currently being used are reductive and do not allow for the complexities of artistic practice and ways of knowing. Boughton maintains that content and pedagogy need to be reconstructed. At the same time, there needs to be a revision of the forms of assessment that will facilitate these changes. "If we want students to engage with personal interests, relevant to their lives, we need to create an assessment structure that not only accommodates individual pursuit of ideas, but also actively promotes it" (268). Universalism runs counter to the interests of students and to the value art education brings to student learning and achievement, including imagination, personally and relevant lived experiences and interests, and critical engagement with ideas.

However, quantification is not the only method that imposes standardization and universalization. The literature on qualitative assessment also supports criterion-based models of practice (see Blaikie, 2001; Dorn, 2003). While educators advocate student self-assessment, for example, as more holistic and student-centered, the pressure towards greater teacher/school accountability has resulted in fewer teachers implementing these less regulated forms of assessment.

Imbricated within a universalist argument is an approach to teaching and learning grounded in Cartesian dualistic thought, where the mind and body are divisible and separate. Vision has traditionally been associated with the mind and conscious reason. To see, to know, and to understand, are bound within vision's mastery over an object, reducing knowledge to the acquisition of form (Foti, 2003; Vasseleu, 1998). In art education, given the profundity of the visual, this mode of thinking has dominated perception and informs the field's understanding and practice of curriculum and assessment. Aesthetic judgment that follows this Cartesian split is trapped in the belief in the autonomous rational subject, which is separated from the object(s) of perception. Rigorous standardized assessment isolates and separates components and does not take into account bodied subjectivity in the meaning-making process. Although postmodernist theories, including feminism and post-structuralism, have advocated a shift towards the value of subjectivity within learning and knowing, assessment has been slow to embrace this paradigm shift. While postmodern concerns have been addressed (although in many cases in a limited fashion) in terms of content (i.e., multicultural and antioppressive curricula), rarely have they been taken up with regards to assessment. Implementing a rationalist approach to education disembodies, disengages, and dehumanizes subjects.

However, many art educators have sought ways to counter this rational, objective paradigm. Instead they opt for assessment models based on creativity, personal expression, and artistic intent assessing student performance often through process alone. While admirable in their attempt to assert meaning over form, such strategies also continue to disembody art practices maintaining that meaning is made not through connections with others, but is located in the autonomous self, where individual consciousness is viewed as private, self-contained, and invisible. The formation of existence, consciousness, is removed from contact with other minds or bodies and it is perceived as "outside" of space and time.

While the regulation of assessment practices is problematic in its own right, my concern with standardization is not limited to defining specific criteria or rubrics. Rather, what I object to are assessment models that continue to delimit the body's role in the production of knowledge. Reducing understanding and knowing to universal categories negates epistemological differences that feminist scholars have fought so hard to make visible and salient. Therefore, when we structure assessment models on the assumption that all teachers will teach in given ways, and that all students regardless of race, class, gender in addition to life encounters, experiences, and personal interests are the same, we fail to address a politics of difference in knowing, seeing, ways of understanding, and lived experience. In fact, my arguments are directed not only towards standardized assessment models, which include both paper-pencil tests and qualitative methods such as portfolio assessment, but to all types of assessment that perpetuate a mind/body split through the regulation, control, and classification of bodies and knowledges.

The Fragmentation of Curriculum and Pedagogy

Reflecting on curriculum standards, Brent Wilson (1996) offers yet another argument when he writes: "the most severe failing of the National Standards for Arts Education is that the individual standards do not form a coherent vision of the purposes of arts education" (3). Student performance cannot be measured by the assessment of individual parts that are detached from the complexities of artistic practice. If educators continue to administer the standards point by point, they "would hopelessly and unnecessarily fragment arts education" (Wilson, 1996, 3). Wilson maintains that standards have little or no value when they stand-alone. Rather, they are intended to be interconnected, and "when combined, form the complex acts of artistic creation, performance, critical interpretation, and judgment" (3). This sentiment is echoed by Felicity Haynes (1996), who claims that assessment is unable to cope with the complexity, ambiguity, and uncertainty of artistic learning. Yet preservice teacher preparation programs and the political movement to chart and regulate teacher accountability enforce this fragmentation.

In both British Columbia, where I taught in the teacher education program at the University of British Columbia, and at Penn State University, where I am currently an assistant professor, student teachers are often required to isolate individual standards for each and every lesson or unit plan. More importantly rather than conceptualizing a lesson around issues, contexts, and themes that explore arts in relation to social action and student understanding, and/or critically examine human assumptions and values, student teachers have been instructed to list lesson outcomes and objectives through standard-based approaches at the outset of creating a lesson plan. Students have been instructed to prepare a lesson by starting with a list of standards and outcomes. Assessment has then been reduced to a set of graded points measuring the standards against student-produced work. The debasement of teaching and learning to static labels (9.1.12C—integrate advanced vocabulary into the art forms, or 2.3—measurement and estimation: proportion and scale) is detrimental to embodied, critical learning where students become active agents in learning and knowing.

Fragmentation also leads to complicated, time-consuming, and arduous planning and implementation. Student teachers spend hours poring over curriculum documents to link their lesson plans to components within the standards. In effect, student teachers end up with a shopping list of standards that are empty signifiers and serve only as vague placeholders for teacher accountability. While teachers find lack of time and resources problematic in constructing an effective assessment model, due in part to large class sizes and limited scheduled art classes in the week, teachers and student teachers alike tell me that they spend the majority of their time locating and organizing which standards "fit" their lesson plan. Accountability is not concerned with learning, but about controlling what we teach and the minds of our teachers and students.

Arguably, any lesson plan can "fit" various standards, given their ambiguous language and open possibilities. For instance, the Pennsylvania Arts and Humanities Standard 9.1.12.J states that students will analyze and evaluate the use of traditional and contemporary technologies for producing performing and exhibiting works in the arts. While many educators argue that these standards are open and thus, each individual teacher has the autonomy to work within the framework as they see fit, I concur with Wilson (1996) who contends that they emphasize and imply that artistic practices can be understood through individual parts rather than as a whole. While common sense posits meaning as a linear assemblage, as something that is added to and built upon using discrete and isolated parts, artistic ways of knowing are more aligned with what French philosopher Jean Luc Nancy (2000) articulates when he writes that meaning is created when meaning "comes apart" (2). Regardless of whether a student has engaged in the process of creating a painting, drawing, or a performative intervention, fragmenting learning and knowing into a series of parts fails to grasp interconnected and folded relationships—the in-between. Rather we need to consider learning and knowing from the position of the fold. A fold is both exterior and interior. In a fold inside and outside remain distinct, but not separate; rather they are doubled. Un/folding is not the reverse of a fold, but may result in additional folds. Thus, the fold appears interconnected, embracing touch and intercorporeality. The condition of the fold is the premise that it is not a void or an absence in the sense of nothing. Rather the fold is being turned back on itself—touching.

Deleuze (1993) translates the fold as sensuous vibrations, a world made up of divergent series, an infinity of pleats and creases. Un/folding divides endlessly, folds within folds touching one another. "Matter thus offers an infinitely porous, spongy, or cavernous texture without emptiness, caverns endlessly contained in other caverns" (5). Challenging Descartes, Deleuze is mindful of the fold as matter that cannot be divided into separable parts. A fold is not divisible into independent points, but rather any un/folding results in additional folds; it is the movement or operation of one fold to another. "The division of the continuous must not be taken as sand dividing into grains, but as that of a sheet of paper or of a tunic in fold, in such a way that an infinite number of folds can be produced. . .without the body ever dissolving into point or minima. A fold is always folded within a fold" (6). Perception is not a question then of part to whole but a singular totality "where the totality can be as imperceptible as the parts" (87).

Understanding is not embodied in perceiving the sum of all parts, rather it is distinguished by and within the fold. Assessment practices need to be reconstructed from the perspective of the fold, where learning and knowing are interconnected and embodied. In other words, assessment in visual art needs to recognize the multi-layered structures of meaning.

Formalism and the Isolated Art Object

A third issue and concern with assessment models and practices is the belief that the art product a student creates can be used as the basis for assessing student performance (Blaikie, 2001; Rush, 1996). This suggests that art can be quantified outside of any contextual understanding. This approach, while fragmentary, also reduces art and assessment to formalist understandings—for example, the elements and principles of design. In a survey conducted by Stanley Madeja, Charles Dorn, and Robert Sabol, ninety percent of the teachers considered the elements and principles of design to be essential to learning in art (Madeja, 2004). Similarly, Blaikie's (2001) findings support assessment models based on the elements and principles of design, where emphasis is placed on studio work. Most assessment practices adopted by classroom teachers and policy-makers, who create standardized tests, are empirically based and rely heavily on formalist elements, allowing little room for expressive outcomes including aesthetic qualities and problem-solving abilities. While art history and criticism comprises a part of the art curriculum, assessment is often limited to the studio product as a composite of student knowledge. For instance, criticism is often reduced to peer and class critiques of student-produced work.

This model emphasizes a static and isolated art object that is distant and separated from artistic ways of knowing, lived subjective experience, and critical social action. As Boughton (2004) so aptly argues: "A curriculum based upon the acquisition of facts, media skills, and knowledge of form cannot satisfy the central questions of value that must be addressed in a visual culture program" (266). He continues, admonishing arts curricula that reify standardization:

> An art curriculum should not be thought of as a body of knowledge, pre-defined in quantifiable chunks, taught systematically in sequential units, so that it can be measured by multiple-choice tests. Nor should it be thought of as a sequence of traditional art media-based activities that require students to produce similar objects skillfully. (267)

Thus, in order to sustain visual art's complexity, the homogenization, reduction, and distillation of form must be addressed. "We need to think again about the value of diversity in the arts, the central place of imagination in the education of our students, and the importance of dealing with the values implied by seductive art forms" (Boughton, 2004, 267). Assessment cannot become a series of separated points, sanitized, and devoid of interconnected meanings. Similarly, the studio product is not sufficient in itself to assert student understanding and learning.

What educators need to embrace is the uncertainty and unknowingness of visual art, and teaching and learning. Instead of favoring terms such as creativity, imagination, and talent, educators would be better served if they begin to address learning and knowing (and for that matter teaching) as acts of becoming, where through perceiving, responding, making, and critically analyzing subjects perform themselves into being (Deleuze & Guattari, 1987; Garoian, 1999; Grosz, 1994). Regardless of subject area, but certainly within the visual arts, recognizing that learning and knowing are not discrete objects that can be divisible into parts is paramount to a postmodern education that asserts subjectivity, personal and social action, and critical engagement through meaning making as essential aspects of knowing and being. Educators and policy-makers alike need to recognize the complexities, ambiguities, and vulnerabilities of understanding, learning, and knowing as bodied encounters, where meaning is made between being(s)-in-relation, intertwined and interconnected (Springgay, 2004a).

IMAG(E)INING A RELATIONAL ARTS CURRICULUM

Instead of creating assessment models in the arts that exemplify and reify objectification and standardization, teaching and learning would benefit from an approach to assessment that ruptures vision with touch; an approach that understands assessment as living inquiry, where the making and responding to works of art become bodied visual encounters. In order to think through this space of living inquiry, I am going to discuss a research project that I conducted within a secondary school in a large urban city in Canada (see Springgay, 2004a; in press). I was invited to this school as a visiting artist-researcher-teacher, where I created and implemented a six-month curriculum project that examined youth understandings and negotiations of body knowledge in and as visual culture.

The study took place two days a week during class time, although I was present in the school to work with students during lunch hours, after school, and during spare classes most days during the week. The curriculum project was structured around the themes body surfaces, body encounters, and body sites, and students engaged in critical discussions and art-making as a way of thinking through the body in and as visual culture. Emphasis was placed on contemporary forms of art including installation, new media, and performance. Rather than a curriculum composed of discrete parts, where students are expected to create art products, teaching and learning as living inquiry understands knowing and being as a space of interrogation (de Cosson, et. al., in press; Springgay, et. al., in press; Springgay, 2003, 2004a, 2004b). In other words perceiving, responding, questioning, and creating works of art become moments of personal and social reflection, where students and teachers interrogate what it means to know, to learn, and to be active citizens in the world.

Touch as a way of knowing challenges the mechanisms of visual perception. As a way of knowing, sensory experiences are expressed with, in, and through the body. Unlike vision, which is distant and separate, touch as a contact sense forms a proximal understanding between subject(s) and object(s). Touch is not only a physical materialization of skin on matter but attends to an awareness of our body in relation to other bodies and objects. Touch materializes as a concept whereby we come to experience and to know through the body as living experience and in proximity. Tactile epistemologies inform how we experience body knowledges as encounters between being(s)-in-relation.

The ambiguity of the term *touch* resides in the fact that it embodies multiple meanings. For instance, it can refer to a particular sense—touch, but it is also employed as a concept that envelopes all the senses simultaneously—vision, taste, smell, sound and touch. Thus, touch becomes a perception that resonates with multiple sensory knowing, often referred to as synesthesia. In other contexts, it refers to encounters between things, and the permeability and un/folding of interior and exterior, often described as intercorporeality. All these meanings are contingent on the concepts of proximity and relationality. Rather than separating each interpretation from the other, I prefer to tangle these meanings together, complexifying touch. This complexity is important because it embodies the equivocation of body knowledge.

Often tactile epistemologies are difficult to translate to the written word. Many scholars treat tactile knowledge as prediscursive and hence natural. This is a position I dispute. Rather, tactile epistemologies penetrate our bodies; they are inside the visible, un/folding but never fully becoming an object (Merleau-Ponty, 1968). This visceral philosophical space is not an unconscious act of self-expression, but rather a language full of intention, a latent ambiguity that materializes and is cultivated as body knowledge; the body in the world, active and aware.

The translation of this tactile epistemology to assessment is a difficult task, one that attests to a kind of elliptical morphology where neither language (assessment) nor art is completely transparent or opaque but rather there is a slippage that always alludes to hesitation, nervousness, and discomfort. In this way, the continual process of art-making and un/folding enables, or one might even say, forces a constant interrogation, to pry open assessment practices, and to allow the inquiry to penetrate deeply—to be touched.

Assessment practices, I argue, must embrace tactile epistemologies asking students to think through the body in and as visual culture. In doing so assessment becomes embodied, folded, and interconnected with aspects of learning and knowing with, in, and through visual art. To contextualize this reconceptualization of assessment I will highlight one example from the research study *Inside the Visible* (see Springgay, 2004a). Note in the following account that the email address is fabricated.

One of the students generated an email exchange that questioned and examined how we come to know and experience emotions as bodied encounters (see Springgay, in press). Andrew (a pseudonym) created an email that he sent to a number of anonymous addresses through list serves. The email was a vague attempt at forgiveness and he signed the email using only the initials MH.

> I guess we all have things we'd rather have forgiven. I think in this case we all agree that it'd be best to just drop this here and now, and move on. Personally, I'm willing to forgive anyone if they'll forgive me. It seems like we've all just kind of fallen into something none of us want, and it also doesn't look like we're ever gonna figure it out. My vote's for just moving on. Things can only go up from here. Anyway, keep up the correspondence.—MH

Many people responded to the email asking Andrew if he could remind them of the wrongdoing that had necessitated the email in the first place, or alerting him to the fact that they had received the email in error.

M,

Why are you writing me, re: forgiveness, which is of course the doorway to all inner spaciousness and freedom. I don't know you.
C

From :
To :   "Marty Holsten" <martyholsten@hotmail.com>
Subject :   Re: Apologies/Forgivness
Date :   Mon, 14 Apr 2003 12:33:00 -0800

Hi Marty—thank you for your apology/forgiveness but I'm drawing a blank about what this is about? I just wanted to tell you that I'm not sidestepping your words—my computer system crashed and I'm only now getting it back into gear and back on line. Movin' on is what life is about—but of course, we carry what we've learned and experienced always within the molecules of our bodies—best to make peace always!
L

Ironically the personal responses caused Andrew to feel guilty for having invaded people's email space. As a result, Andrew composed yet another email, which he sent to the respondents, disclosing the nature of the project and asking for forgiveness himself. This prompted yet another set of emails back and forth on the nature of guilt and forgiveness. Throughout this email-generated art project Andrew discussed his ideas, thoughts, emotions, and negotiated this learning space with fellow classmates. The work of art did not reside only in the text/image created on the computer screen, but in the bodied exchange between participants and the students as Andrew began to interrogate and question these encounters of meaning making.

This project, like many others created throughout the term, doesn't allow for standard assessment practices, where students submit a completed art product for assessment. While arguably issues of form are present, they cannot be isolated from the contextual aspect of the work, and the embodied relational acts of interrogation. Meaning and form cannot be separated or objectified. Similarly, Andrew did not present his work to the class through the traditional auspices of a studio critique, where the isolated art object is subjected to moments of reflection. Rather student understandings, subjectivities, critical reflection, and art-making are folded together.

Andrew did not create a draft that he presented to the teacher and his classmates for critique and feedback, nor did he gather a portfolio of works in progress to assist in assessment. Rather the evolution of the work, the directions, challenges that he faced, and his negotiation of embodied emotional knowing were constructed between self and other, mutually interrogating and confronting each other. If we are submerged in an understanding of identity that is static and fixed, isolated from any relation to others, we neglect knowledge that is formed in relation to others. Therefore, relational knowing is necessary for personal and social reconstruction and transformation.

As the term progressed, Andrew would meet with various classmates to discuss his work, sometimes as a formal class discussion session facilitated by the teacher. This process of interrogation was central to the curriculum project and admittedly at first, a practice that the students struggled against in its unfamiliarity. However, as the artist-researcher-teacher I created situations, both whole class, small group, and individual, where students were forced to pry open the site of meaning making. Students became actively aware of the uncertainty and hesitancy of this process, and confronted learning as "un/knowing" (de Cosson, 2003; Springgay, 2004a). Students were encouraged to seek questions not answers, to stitch, and cut, and felt together new possibilities.

When Andrew received the initial responses to the first email he started to feel guilty for having invaded what he saw as people's private space—their personal email addresses. At the same time, Andrew was uncertain what meanings could be generated from this exchange (the exchange being his artistic act), how to begin interpreting them, or what directions to take. Instead of objectifying the initial email as an "art product" that could be submitted to a classroom teacher for assessment, the concept of an exchange became the central focus of the artistic practice, where meaning making and assessment became imbricated and interwoven. Andrew was encouraged to think through bodied encounters as spaces of potential learning and knowing, to question and to challenge the artistic sites as moments of personal and social agency.

So how did Andrew and I, as the teacher, assess his learning? Students were encouraged to move beyond an understanding of visual art as an object towards examining visual art and culture as spaces of interrogation, where meanings are formed between things. This relationality became a pedagogical site of meaning making in the classroom. Instead of presenting his email project as an art object, Andrew and classmates were encouraged to view their various artistic encounters, which included visual journals, drawing, painting, installation, textile pieces, video work, and performance art as intercorporeal sites of meaning making, where learning and understanding with, in, and through visual art became embodied encounters and exchanges. Assessment could not be attached to the end of the unit, nor could it amass itself through the evaluation of discrete and separate parts, rather assessment was folded into and through the artistic acts. Assessment through touch forms a relational understanding between curriculum and pedagogy. Students were encouraged to understand art and art practices as interrogation—a space of critical examination of how we come to know and how this knowing effects our subject position in the world.

This pedagogical practice moves students from knowledge about form (elements and principles of design), towards a greater understanding of the connections between meaning and form as living inquiry, and a reconsideration of the ways in which student art develops subjectivity and acts as cultural critique (Freedman, 2003a; 2003b). Assessment needs to ask questions about the complexities of creating, interrogating, and thinking through art as bodied visual encounters. This requires that curriculum and pedagogy, not just assessment undergo a significant shift. Kerry Freedman (2003b), Doug Boughton (2004), David Darts (2004), Kevin Tavin (2003), and others consider this paradigm shift an essential part of the movement towards visual culture as art education, where teaching and learning reside in the intersections between "the visual" and student identity, subjectivity, and cultural critique. This follows feminist practices that recognize visual culture as constitutive of culture where visual meaning is a relational play and living inquiry becomes a process of reimaging and transforming personal and social change (Meskimmon, 2003; Rogoff, 2000). Art is not a static object, illustrative of cultural conditions, but rather becomes an act of interrogation that provokes shifts in cultural consciousness. This perspective invites participants to actively engage in the collectivity of the process. Art becomes places of struggle, where meaning making is hesitant and confusing, a place of penetration and deep inquiry. Art is a way of knowing and being in its own right.

Our failure to generate best practices in assessment, I believe, is because we continue to separate and disembody assessment from curriculum and pedagogy. Similarly, we continue to reify the art object as a symbol of student learning. If students are to expand their knowledge of self and other, and the world through the creation, performance, and critical interrogation of art, then assessment in art education needs to be reconstructed alongside teaching and learning, where all aspects of meaning making are understood as living inquiry. Learning must move towards a relational aesthetic, where knowing and understanding exist in the fold.

WORKS CITED

Bensur, B. 2002. "Frustrated Voices of Art Assessment." *Art Education,* 55(6): 18–23.

Blaikie, F. 2001. "Strategies for Studio Art Assessment in Canada." In *Readings in Canadian Art Teacher Education. Second Edition.* R. L. Irwin and K. Grauer, eds. 199–219. London, Ontario: Canadian Society for Education Through Art.

Boughton, D. 2004. "The Problem of Seduction: Assessing Visual Culture." *Studies in Art Education,* 45(3): 265–69.

Boughton, D., E. Eisner, and J. Ligtvoet (eds.). 1996. *Evaluating and Assessing the Visual Arts in Education* New York: Teachers College Press.

Darts, D. 2004. "Visual Culture Jam: Art, Pedagogy, and Creative Resistance." *Studies in Art Education,* 45(4): 315–30.

de Cosson, A. 2003. *(Re)searching sculpted a/r/tography: (Re)learning subverted-knowing through aporetic praxis.* Doctoral Dissertation. Vancouver, BC: University of British Columbia.

de Cosson, A., R. Irwin., S. Kind, and S. Springgay. (In press.) "Walking in wonder: Encountering the visual in living inquiry." In *The Art of visual inquiry,* edited by A. Cole, G. Knowles, and T. Luciani. New Brunswick: Backalong Books.

Deleuze, G. 1993. *The Fold: Leibniz and the Baroque.* Minneapolis, MN: University of Minnesota Press.

Deleuze, G., and F. Guattari. 1987. *A Thousand plateaus: Capitalism and schizophrenia.* Minneapolis, MN: University of Minnesota Press.

Dorn, C. 2003. "Models for assessing art performance (MAPP): A K–12 Project." *Studies in Art Education,* 44(4): 350–371.

Eisner, E. 1999. "The National Assessment in the Visual Arts." *Arts Education Policy Review,* 100(6): 16–20.

Foti, V. 2003. *Visions Invisibles: Philosophical Explorations.* Albany, NY: State University of New York Press.

Freedman, K. 2003a. "The Importance of Student Artistic Production to Teaching Visual Culture." *Art Education,* 56(2): 38–43.

———. 2003b. *Teaching Visual Culture: Curriculum, Aesthetics, and the Social Life of Art.* New York: National Art Education Association.

Garoian, C. 1999. *Performing Pedagogy: Toward an Art of Politics*. Albany, NY: State University of New York Press.

Grosz, E. 1994. *Volatile bodies*. Bloomington, IN: Indiana University Press.

Hanley, B. 2003. "Policy Issues in Arts Assessment in Canada: 'Let's Get Real.'" *Arts Education Policy Review*, 105(1): 33–38.

Haynes, F. 1996. "Zero Plus One: Evaluation and Assessment in the Visual Arts." In *Evaluating and Assessing the Visual Arts in Education*. D. Boughton, E. Eisner, and J. Ligtvoet, eds. 27–41. New York: Teachers College Press.

Madeja, S. 2004. "Alternative Assessment Strategies for Schools." *Arts Education Policy Review*, 105(5): 3–13.

Merleau-Ponty, M. 1968. *The Visible and the Invisible*. Translated by Alphonso Lingis. Evanston: Northwestern University Press.

Meskimmon, M. 2003. *Women Making Art: History, Subjectivity, Aesthetics*. New York: Routledge.

Nancy, J. L. 2000. *Of Being Singular Plural*. Stanford, CA: Stanford University Press.

Rogoff, I. 2000. *Terra Infirma: Geography's Visual Culture*. London, UK: Routledge.

Rush, J. 1996. "Conceptual Consistency and Problem Solving: Tools to Evaluate Learning in Studio Art." In *Evaluating and assessing the visual arts in education*. D. Boughton, E. Eisner, and J. Ligtvoet, eds. 42–53. New York: Teachers College Press.

Springgay, S. 2003. "Cloth as Intercorporeality: Touch, Fantasy, and Performance and the Construction of Body Knowledge." *International Journal of Education and the Arts*, 4(5). http://ijea.asu.edu/v4n5/.

———. 2004a. "Inside the Visible: Youth Understandings of Body Knowledge Through Touch." Doctoral dissertation. Vancouver, BC: The University of British Columbia.

———. 2004b. "Inside the Visible: Arts-based Educational Research as Excess." *Journal of Curriculum and Pedagogy*, 1 (1):8–18. Image selected for cover of journal.

———. (In press). "Thinking Through Bodies: Bodied Encounters and the Process of Meaning Making in an email Generated Art Project." *Studies in Art Education*.

Springgay, S., R. L. Irwin., and S. Wilson Kind. (In press). "A/r/tography as Living Inquiry Through Art and Text." *Qualitative Inquiry*, 11 (4).

Tavin, K. 2003. "Wrestling with Angels, Searching for Ghosts: Toward a Critical Pedagogy of Visual Culture." *Studies in Art Education*, 44(3): 197–213.

Vasseleu, C. 1998. *Textures of Light: Vision and Touch in Irigaray, Levinas and Merleau-Ponty*. New York: Routledge.

Wilson, B. 1996. "Arts Standards and Fragmentation: A Strategy for Holistic Assessment." *Arts Education Policy Review*, 98(2), 2–9.

Chapter 8

Finding Balance and Embodiment in Arts Assessment with "No Child Left Behind"

Renée Kredell

As Maxine Greene (1996) states, "I am who I am not yet," implying thereby that we inhabit a space of ongoing becoming. As physical bodies, we live in an unsettled space that houses and engenders our capacity to interpret and transform our world. Our bodies are sites of transition and transformation. They transition naturally on their own; they offer us an opportunity to make comparisons between what was, and what is. By their own inherent, irrepressible dynamism, they drive toward various forms of transition, compelling thereby the work of comparison, differentiation, and evaluation. In doing so, they offer countless opportunities to probe the likenesses and differences between what was and what is, as well as between what is and what might yet be.

Embodied beings are always integral parts of a personal and cultural continuum in which unpredictable disruptions, reversals, arrests, and discontinuities of various sorts are unavoidable. As physical entities, living forms, animate beings, we are in a process of becoming: as is evident (to take but several examples) in the aging process, in our vacillations between health and illness, and the transformation born of the conflict between prior understandings and present exigencies. This transitional space is a liminal space between, above all else, "what we are" and "what we are not yet."

The anthropologist Victor Turner (1969) characterizes liminal spaces as "neither here nor there; they are betwixt and between" (95). It is within these liminal spaces where learning occurs most dramatically and deeply, in particular, in those transitions involving reflective perceptions noticed and articulated primarily through the sentient, intelligent body-mind (Dewey, 1925). This is an unsettled space where gathering of perceptions and ideas occurs within sustained or momentary transitional episodes or crises moments; it is in this liminal space where embodied assessment most appropriately and effectively takes place.

To negotiate our world we exist within a dual liminality: (1) our own transitional bodies themselves and (2) the relationship of those bodies to the outside world within its own constantly shifting scenes of negotiation. As communal beings, we align ourselves to institutional and social values, in the hopes of establishing a progressive humanistic society that functions as a collective. If we did not align cooperatively as a society, assessment would remain an individual self-reflexive process carried out in personal liminal spaces between (1) mind/body, spirit/body, knowledge/body, and (2) their relationships to the world. If we existed exclusively as unrelated atomistic individuals, the outcome of these dual reflexive processes would be for the sole benefit of the self. But since we do participate in a community as citizens, we begin to infringe upon a very tangled dialogue of accountability. The threads of this dialogue knot around the following constructs: what forms of knowledge are privileged and by implication what forms are discounted or discredited; who is accountable to whom; what knowledge should be measured? Here is where we must begin to untangle the challenges embedded in the assessment dialogue.

WHAT KNOWLEDGE IS PRIVILEGED IN PUBLIC EDUCATION?

In Chapter 7, Springgay argues that "assessment practices must embrace tactile epistemologies asking students to think through the body in and as visual culture." Her argument does not explore the boundaries in our current educational regime that restrict embodied assessment: the reinstatement of curriculum, pedagogy, and assessment based in traditional theories and goals in the form of governmental educational mandates. This piece aligns with her hope for embodied assessment, but desires to articulate some of the restrictive policies that make the implementation of such strategies a more complicated endeavor than she suggests.

Ideally, we all hope to move in the direction of embodied learning and assessment experiences but we cannot go forward and speak accurately about arts assessment, unless we outline the political framework delimiting current assessment and directly influencing our ability as art educators to teach and assess art in an embodied way. We must pause to picture the assessment theory and practice divide as it lays itself out as an assortment of disparate objectives. We cannot effectively enter into this dialogue about theoretical/philosophically based holistic (mind/body) arts assessment strategies without being aware of federally mandated assessment initiatives that make the use of the terms *embodied, holistic,* and *liminal* stand out like sixties drug paraphernalia in a church rummage sale.

Within the current K–12 American curriculum we are challenged by the governmental directive of No Child Left Behind (NCLB). President Bush signed this educational reform initiative into law on January 8, 2002. This directive requires that public schools become accountable for the education of all students based on the same standards to be met on the same timetable. Schools must show increased test scores, adequate yearly progress (AYP) over a two-year time frame, or meet the following consequences: (a) closure, and to be reopened as a charter school; (b) replacement of all staff whose students failed to make AYP; (c) hiring a for-profit management company, or (d) yielding to a state takeover (Chapman, 2005, 9).

To avoid these consequences, ninety to one hundred percent of students must score "proficient or above" in reading, mathematics, and science by 2014 (Chapman, 2005, 7). Robert Linn, president of the American Educational Research Association, estimates that "half of public schools will be subjected to AYP sanctions even if they make dramatic improvements" (Chapman, 2005, 11). Because this directive is aligned to the core standards, quantifiable, factual knowledge is privileged over qualitative knowledge. To enter into a singular dialogue of embodied assessment seems fanciful and unrealistic, when the reality of the K–12 system is that teachers and administrators are fighting to meet the guidelines of NCLB and struggling to drill the required knowledge based on national and state standards into students to meet the obligatory goals. Pausing to reflect about a liminal space of assessment, even though this is where we should aim to be, does not fit into this current educational picture. Where would the current art educator, postcertification, be introduced to a holistic embodied arts assessment strategy under the current regime? Certainly not through district-funded inservices that are focused on meeting the NCLB mandates.

This education reform should signal to those interested in the balance between traditional and critical theory in educational institutions, a return to policy based on the tenets of traditional theory. Kathleen Weiler in her book, *Women Teaching for Change* (1988), outlines the objectives of traditional and then critical educational goals in the following way:

> In general, traditional educational theory has taken the existing arrangement of society as given, not changeable in any serious way, and desirable. . . Reforms are seen as adjustments of a fundamentally sound system of the social allocation of human beings. (5)

On the other hand, "what essentially defines critical educational theory is its moral imperative and its emphasis on the need for both individual empowerment and social transformation. That is, it emphasizes the need to develop critical consciousness in students as well as the need to change society as it is presently arranged" (Weiler, 1988, 4–6).

The teeter-totter of educational reform hovers between the recurring tides of traditional and critical theoretical reform initiatives, most often settling back into tenets of traditional theory and its modernist notions of factual, fixed, certain knowledge sets. This is where embodied learning is pushed aside for the depositing of a series of factual knowledge sets (Freire, 2002, 72). The pedagogical and assessment dialogues hover between the factual preservation of current knowledge, for instance, curricula based solely on the elements and principles of design, versus art curricula that promote personal empowerment, the investigation into power structures, and social transformation, aligned to dialogues within visual culture or critical theory. This divide illustrates why an embodied assessment strategy is a foreign system within a traditional theoretical educational model. There is a need for educational institutions, generating our future educators, to sustain substantive dialogues about the social/political basis of educational and assessment models that originate from both theoretical foundations. Only with the understanding of how both theoretical models manifest in school reform, pedagogy, and assessment will teachers, functioning as intellectuals be able to navigate and alter these systems (Giroux, 1988, 126). Equipped with this knowledge, teachers will be able to ride the fluctuating tide between conservative and progressive political agendas.

WHO IS ACCOUNTABLE TO WHOM?

No Child Left Behind forces not only the traditional core subjects of language arts, math, and science to align with state and national standards, but also the arts. As administrators struggle to keep their student population meeting the mandated requirements, programs that are not seen as mandatory are cut or resources relocated. Art programs risk downsizing or elimination if not deemed as necessary to help meet the goals of No Child Left Behind mandates (Chapman, 2005, 14). Whereas art is already struggling to maintain its subject area position in virtually any basic curriculum, No Child Left Behind has art teachers scrambling to advocate for their curriculum as valuable and necessary by showing how it can support a child's "core subject areas" through its own alignment to standards. Arts standards become the marker for accountability, whether or not we are currently pleased with their scope and content.

In higher education, at the preservice teacher level, here is where we again meet the theory/practice divide. We may be ambivalent toward standards-based art education and assessment, but this is what the current regime supported by NCLB requires. As a solution to this current situation, I propose it is necessary to teach student teachers the language of the standards as a political tool to function within the current system, along with the traditional assessment tools such as formative and summative assessment strategies and rubrics that stem naturally from standards-based art education. The ability to produce assessment data using these standards-based tools is art education's closest approach to quantitative assessment but should not be our sole assessment response.

In addition to the standards-based assessment strategies however, arts educators need to develop embodied assessment strategies that can originate from the dialogues of performance art, reflective practice, and performance. Performance art can be a medium for students to conceptualize their understandings or impasses through the body as medium. Through engagements in reflective practice, students can be asked to participate in sustained reflective dialogues through performative and/or visual art interactions over time creating a series of embodied responses as assessment. Performance-based tasks such as plays, pantomime, and rituals also allow students to synthesize, conceptualize, rehearse, and then perform embodied reflective assessments based on unsettled disparities, ideas, and/or ideologies. Current and future teachers must be capable of understanding how to protect and defend arts education through support of the current system, while at the same time enhancing and challenging it through more holistic assessment and pedagogical strategies, that recognizes, as Springgay writes in her chapter, "the multi-layered structures of meaning."

As an instructor who has taught both education and art education preservice teachers, I feel it is necessary to educate students regarding the political power that standards hold, both for and against students, and their capacity to both sustain and destroy the integrity of an art education program, while at the same time introducing student teachers to the possibilities of embodied assessment. The clarity that needs to surface within this dialogue is to encourage the teacher as intellectual to use the understanding of the standards as a political tool to empower the value of arts in education while still creating unsettled places of learning and assessment (Giroux, 1988, 126). I maintain that the call for a standardized educational system will always exist and that the solution to this conundrum is a mediated, liminal space that exists somewhere between compliance and subversion.

WHAT KNOWLEDGE SHOULD BE MEASURED?

Art has always struggled to define what it has been, what it now is, and what it might most fruitfully become. From this fluctuating dialogue, the discipline of art for educational curriculum is derived. Especially in its most contemporary forms art is an interrogation of the meaning of art itself. As we try to articulate the purpose of assessment, we confront the task of defining the knowledge, practices, and philosophical constructs that should be taught and then assessed. Here again we must ask ourselves, who is accountable to whom? Whose definition of art becomes the body of knowledge to be used as a basis to create curriculum and then assessments?

As art educators answer this question, we must first separate current institutional requirements and definitions of art from our own comprehensive definition of art. From this delineation we then can devise assessment strategies that fulfill both frameworks while at the same time providing art education that is both critical and meaningful to students. As art educators we need to be engaged in a constant search for the shifting body of knowledge that should comprise art education curriculum. Second, we need to ask how we can document the growth attained through that curriculum via meaningful assessment tools that support the ever-changing curriculum and the unsettled body as a liminal site.

The subversion of the current mandated testing measures can be achieved by finding ways to help students see the liminal-relational spaces between the knowledge that is being professed as "core" and the knowledge that does not fit within the quantitative boundaries. In addition, students should explore the liminal sites within and outside their own bodies. Assisting students to be accountable to themselves for the translation of and reflection on their world and its often-fixed knowledge systems is the key to meeting and subverting the traditional accountability system.

CONCLUSION

> It is our inward journey that leads us through time—forward or back, seldom in a straight line, most often spiraling. Each of us is moving, changing, with respect to others. (Welty, 1985, 102)

No Child Left Behind provides one endpoint in contrast to our hopes of a holistic embodied assessment. Betwixt and between these two markers is a liminal space that can be explored to produce new knowledge about assessment and to further define what information should articulate the discipline of art. The exploration of this space requires that we teach and assess in liminal-unsettled spaces that acknowledge national assessment priorities.

The outcome of teaching an embodied assessment practice would be for each student to become a "know-body"[1] (Colapietro, 2004). This space would situate the individual and collective learners in investigations seeking out the relational discoveries between past and new conceptions. Assessment then becomes a process of critical reflective praxis within an embodied journey, requiring that we use our minds and body through investigations in a "forward or back," "falling out of step and then recovering" journey to reconstruct, reconsider, and resituate the ideas that shape our identity and how we perceive our world (Dewey, 1934, 14). Is not the ultimate goal of assessment the enhancement and thus, inescapably, the transformation of praxis? Educators can expand the classroom from a place that instills knowledge, using the banking method, to a place where reflection yields dynamic meeting points of transformation through the use of embodied pedagogies (Freire, 2002, 72). Nonetheless, embodied assessment theory will always be challenged by policymakers who are invested in traditional theory's reinstatement of the status quo through the reproduction of fixed knowledge sets.

Two thoughts: as Eudora Welty (1985) states, and Dewey (1934) adds, we are all in a process of "moving, changing, with respect to others," while at the same time "falling. . .and. . .recovering." Although we hold onto our hopes, and sustain our embodied theories through practice, we must remain educated and facile to the current national imperatives. Standardized and embodied assessments can coexist within the same classroom. With political understanding of the current educational regime, supplanted by supplementary embodied assessments, the unsettled nature of art and art education can be fully realized.

NOTE

[1] The reframing of the word knowbody to know-body, meaning embodiment and knowledge together, came about in conversation with Vincent Colapietro, Pennsylvania State University, July 2004.

WORKS CITED

Chapman, L. H. 2005. "No Child Left Behind in Art?" *Art Education*, 58(1): 6–16.
Colapietro,V. 2004. Email correspondence to author, July.
Dewey, J. 1925. "Nature, Life & Body-Mind" in *Experience and Nature* (203–43). Open Court Publishing Co.: Illinois.
———. 1934. *Art as Experience*. New York: Berkley Publishing Group.
Freire, P. 2002. *Pedagogy of the Oppressed*. New York: Continuum.
Giroux, H. 1988. *Teachers as Intellectuals: Toward a Critical Pedagogy of Learning*. Westport, CT: Bergin & Garvey.
Greene, M. 1996. Lecture, Louisiana State University, June 27.
Turner, V. 1969. *The Ritual Process: Structure and Anti Structure*. Chicago: Aldine Publishing Company.
Weiler, K. 1988. *Women Teaching for Change: Gender, Class & Power*. Westport, CT: Bergin & Garvey.
Welty, E. 1985. *One Writer's Beginnings*. Boston: G. K. Hall.

Notes on Contributors

Richard Colwell, founder of the *Bulletin of the Council for Research in Music Education* and the *Quarterly*, is professor emeritus at the University of Illinois and the New England Conservatory of Music. He was editor of the *Handbook of Research on Music Teaching and Learning* (Schirmer, 1992) and coeditor, with Carol Richardson, of the *New Handbook of Research on Music Teaching and Learning* (Oxford, 2002). Among his recent publications are *An Orientation to Music Education* with Lizabeth Wing (Prentice Hall, 2004, 3rd ed.) and *The Teaching of Instrumental Music*. He is the editor of *Musical Cognition and Development in Music Teaching* and *Learning and Research Methodologies in Music Teaching and Learning* (Oxford, 2006).

David J. Elliott is Professor of Music and Music Education at New York University. He is the author of *Music Matters: A New Philosophy of Music Education* (1995) and editor of *Praxial Music Education: Reflections and Dialogues* (2005). He has published extensively in the fields of music education philosophy and multicultural music education. Also, he is an award-winning composer/arranger.

Christina Hong is Associate Professor and Executive Head of School, Performing and Screen Arts, Unitec Auckland, New Zealand. She received her Ph.D. from Griffith University, Brisbane, Australia and her M.A. in dance and related arts from Texas Women's University, Denton, Texas. She is an active contributor to the education and qualifications reform agenda in New Zealand. This has included leadership of projects related to national assessment exemplars, the development of qualifications standards, and the writing and implementation of the national K–12 curriculum for the arts in schools. Her current research interests lie in the exposition of dance as a literacy within a conceptualization of multiliteracies, postmodern curriculum, and reflective practitioner praxis in the arts.

Renée Kredell is an instructor of Art and Theatre at Pennsylvania State University. Her research interest is the investigation into, and the creation of performative critical spaces toward the promotion of personal and public reflective engagements. She holds a B.A. in theatre and dance from the University of California, Santa Cruz, and an M.A. in art from California State University–Northridge. She is currently finishing her doctorate in art education at Pennsylvania State University.

Robert J. Landy, Ph.D., RDT/BCT, LCAT is Professor of Educational Theatre and Applied Psychology and Director of the Drama Therapy Program at New York University. A prolific researcher and writer, Landy has published numerous books, articles, and plays in the fields of Drama Education, Musical Theatre, Drama Therapy, and related topics.

Stephanie Springgay is an Assistant Professor of Art Education and Women's Studies at Pennsylvania State University. She completed her Ph.D. at the University of British Columbia. Her dissertation, *Inside the Visible: Youth Understandings of Body Knowledge Through Touch,* examines adolescent experiences of the body in and as visual culture. Her research and artistic explorations focus on issues of relationality and an ethics of embodiment. In addition, as a multi-disciplinary artist working with installation and video-based art, she investigates the relationship between artistic practices and methodologies of educational research.

Philip Taylor is Associate Professor and Program Director in Educational Theatre at New York University. He has written widely on drama and arts education, qualitative research, and reflective praxis. Past books include *Researching Drama and Arts Education: Paradigms and Possibilities, Applied Theatre: Creating Transformative Encounters in the Community, Redcoats and Patriots: Reflective Practice in Drama and Social Studies,* and *The Drama Classroom: Action, Reflection, Transformation.*

Edward C. Warburton, Ed.D., is Assistant Professor of Theater Arts/Dance at the University of California, Santa Cruz. Warburton received early dance training at the North Carolina School of the Arts and danced professionally with American Ballet Theater and

Boston Ballet. He holds master's degrees in technology and arts education, and a doctorate in human development and psychology from Harvard University. He sits on the board of the National Dance Education Organization and is Associate Editor of the *Research in Dance Education* (UK) journal.